STANDING ORDERS

STANDING ORDERS

THE COMMANDS OF JESUS

DAVID M. CONDRON

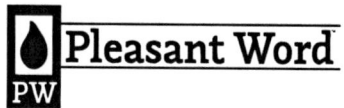

© 2009 by David M. Condron. All rights reserved.

Pleasant Word (a division of WinePress Publishing, PO Box 428, Enumclaw, WA 98022) functions only as book publisher. As such, the ultimate design, content, editorial accuracy, and views expressed or implied in this work are those of the author.

No part of this publication may be reproduced, stored in a retrieval system or transmitted in any way by any means—electronic, mechanical, photocopy, recording or otherwise—without the prior permission of the copyright holder, except as provided by USA copyright law.

The author of this book has waived the publisher's suggested editing and proof reading services. As such, the author is responsible for any errors found in this finished product.

Unless otherwise noted, all Scriptures are taken from the *Holy Bible, New International Version*®, NIV®. Copyright © 1973, 1978, 1984 by the International Bible Society. Used by permission of Zondervan. All rights reserved.

Scripture references marked KJV are taken from the King James Version of the Bible.

Scripture references marked NASB are taken from the New American Standard Bible, © 1960, 1963, 1968, 1971, 1972, 1973, 1975, 1977 by The Lockman Foundation. Used by permission.

ISBN 13: 978-1-4141-1289-3
ISBN 10: 1-4141-1289-0
Library of Congress Catalog Card Number: 2009900536

For Thomas,
who showed me how to follow the Way

Introduction

When I served in the military, the Captain of a ship entrusted the safe operation of the ship to me and the other officers aboard. He placed special trust and confidence in us to carry out his will for the ship and its crew. This was necessary because the Captain could not always be present for every situation. He was human; he too needed to think, rest, and plan for the future.

The task of operating the ship required the constant attention of many people, 24 hours a day, and they all had to work in a coordinated fashion. Simply operating the ship required someone watching to ensure the ship did what the Captain wanted it to do. New situations constantly presented themselves. No day was the same as any other. The Captain used a certain tool to assist his officers in knowing and executing his will for the ship: his Standing Orders.

The Captain's Standing Orders gave general guidance about how he wanted the ship to be driven, what routines the crew should perform at certain times of day, and how to handle various contingencies which may arise. Thus, an officer would always know what the general intentions of the Captain were, and when new situations arose, the officer had some guidance upon which to exercise his judgment. This judgment was the most important aspect of character for a commissioned officer. Being able to make good decisions in various situations allowed the officer to act in the place of the Captain, with his delegated authority accomplishing the Captain's will.

Much of this relationship between Captain and officer is true in the Christian's relationship with the Lord. Jesus has entrusted to his Church very important operations of his Kingdom until he returns. Through his Church, his Father is worshipped in the world. By the Church, people hear the good news of the salvation he won for all at the cross of Calvary. In the Church, the righteous character of his Kingdom can be displayed and contrasted with the wickedness of the selfish world system. In order to accomplish these things, Jesus gave commands to his disciples and told them to teach others "to observe all things that I have commanded you." (Matthew 28:20)

In effect, Jesus has left his Standing Orders for the Church and its operation in a dangerous world so it can accomplish his will until he comes to direct it personally in all his glory. We have been entrusted with more than a multi-million dollar ship; we have been entrusted with the very lives of the people Jesus wants to save. Not only this, he has entrusted us with displaying what his Kingdom is like. In effect, we are ambassadors, just as a country's naval ship can often be used in a diplomatic role as a gesture of goodwill in visiting a far country. The people in that country can see what life in our country is like by meeting and observing us. This is why a Captain always ensures his ship and crew look their best when they make a port call in a foreign land. This is also one reason why Jesus gave us Standing Orders to follow: so we would show those outside the Church what his Kingdom is like.

Many people spend lots of time attempting to discover God's will for their lives. While God does have a specific purpose for each individual, he also has given us Standing Orders as free individuals representing his authority in the world. Whenever life gives us unexpected circumstances, we can look to his Standing Orders and apply the judgment his Holy Spirit is growing in us.

At the end of a designated watch period, another officer would come to the ship's control room and "relieve the watch." The officer who stood the previous watch could now retire in peace for a period of rest while someone else watched over the ship for the Captain. The on-coming watch officer would say: "I relieve you, sir," while the off-going officer would say, "I stand relieved" to signify the transfer of responsibility. By making our decisions in life based on the Standing Orders of Jesus, we have the joy of freely executing his will and we can gladly "stand relieved" at the end of our watch, knowing we have done the best we could to accomplish what he told us to do.

"Whoever has my commands and obeys them, he is the one who loves me. He who loves me will be loved by my Father, and I too will love him and show myself to him."

—John 14:21

"Teaching them to observe all things that I have commanded you."
—Matthew 28:20

So we begin, with God's help.

"Let your light so shine before men, that they may see your good works and glorify your Father in heaven."
—Matthew 5:16

Jesus is speaking to his disciples, the people to whom he is teaching the Sermon on the Mount. He has just explained what life should look like in the kingdom of God. His disciples are encouraged to be humble, meek, hungering for righteousness, merciful, pure, and healers. They are told if anyone sorrows now, it will be made all right in God's kingdom. If they are persecuted now because of doing right, they have an inheritance in God's kingdom and they can be encouraged. He calls such people, "the light of the world." (Matthew 5:14)

The people who display the Kingdom character traits Jesus listed will always be "the light of the world." As we well know, the world is a very dark place. It is a place where it is difficult to trust the motives of other people, a place where you can really get hurt. And how many people combine the quality of hungering for righteousness with mercy, purity, and healing of relationships? It is a rare thing. Usually a "righteous" person becomes very self-righteous, thinking they are better than other people, avoiding other people less "righteous" than themselves. But the "light of the world" people "shine before men" so everyone can see the character of God in them. It is not their own character, but that of God, not their righteousness, but God's. They are full of the same mercy shown to them, not full of themselves.

This kind of person has pure motives. They can look you in the eye and expose themselves with no shame because they have no hidden agendas. They can restore broken relationships because they are willing to take the loss of pride necessary in being the first one to take a step toward reconciliation. They are humble, so there is really nothing to lose by absorbing a hurt to their ego. Security for them is found in the promise of God that the kingdom of heaven is theirs. This is why they can rejoice when people insult them for the sake of Jesus (Matthew 5:12).

Every disciple of Jesus throughout history who reads the Sermon on the Mount has received the same instructions as those original followers on the bank of the Galilean lake. In the same way, Jesus commands us to allow the character of God's kingdom to shine through us. He has a purpose in mind for this command and he even lets us know this purpose. It is so God receives the praise of the men who see His character in us. It will be obvious that *we* could not have this kind of character by ourselves; *nobody* is that good. God will get the glory and people who may have never met God will meet Him through us.

What is our part in all this? The command says, "let your light shine." We have the choice to allow God's character to shine through us. We also can choose to operate from our old selfish motives, hurt pride, desires, and impurity. Our part is to give the Spirit of God the space to work through us and follow His lead. It is hard work in the real world.

Questions:

1. How is your light shining before men now?

2. How are you hiding your light?

3. What is the Holy Spirit leading you to do which you have not yet done?

4. Have you ever prayed for humility, meekness, a hunger for righteousness, mercifulness, purity of heart, or to become a peacemaker?

"Unless your righteousness exceeds the righteousness of the scribes and Pharisees, you will by no means enter the kingdom of heaven."

—Matthew 5:20

Jesus wanted to clear up a very important point for his disciples. He did not come to abolish the Law or the Prophets. Everything God had communicated to Man through history is as true today as it was then. But the *purpose* of the Law and Prophets was a foreshadowing of their completion in the Jewish Messiah, Jesus.

This Messiah is the one who assures us, "until heaven and earth disappear, not the smallest letter, not the least stroke of a pen, will by any means disappear from the Law until everything is accomplished." (Matthew 5:18) What is Jesus commanding us here?

The scribes and Pharisees were so meticulous in their observance of the Law they forgot the real spirit of the Law to focus on the details. Jesus is commanding us not to disregard the Law in our following of him. He is saying, "Look, those scribes and Pharisees have one thing right, at least they have a high regard for obeying God's commands!" The Messiah wants us to have such a regard for God's righteous commands.

The difference between what Jesus wants from us and what the scribes and Pharisees did was Jesus wants us to be full of the spirit without losing attention to the details. He wants us to fulfill the *purpose* of the details in the specific situations we encounter in life. Jesus himself fulfilled the righteous requirements of the Law (Romans 3:21-26) so we can actually taste the righteousness he commanded us to hunger for in the Sermon on the Mount. It is possible, but not in our own strength. By trusting God, we can enter the kingdom of heaven Jesus has described for us. The humility, meekness, righteousness, purity, mercy, and peace can actually be ours, but only if we have more of the Law in us than simply the details.

Without God himself in our lives, we have no hope at all of ever entering the kingdom.

Questions:

1. How has the Law applied to specific situations you have encountered in your life?

2. Have you ever ignored the application of God's Law to yourself?

3. What was the result of ignoring the Law?

4. Have you ever received the righteousness of God which comes through faith in Jesus as Messiah? If so, what brought you to that point? If not, what is keeping you from receiving him?

"Whoever says, 'You fool!' shall be in danger of hell fire."
—Matthew 5:22

How often we treat other people with contempt! We feel justified ourselves in what we are doing, they cross our path, or disagree with us, and we experience conflict. Because we know we are right and they are wrong, we call them all kinds of names, either to their face or to someone else.

Jesus compares this with murder (Matthew 5:21). In his view of the Law, it is the same thing: the destruction of a person by character assassination. He reminds us anyone who says a word of contempt, like "Raca" in Aramaic, the language of his time, is in danger of being judged by the Sanhedrin authority of the time. Even worse, if we call another person "Fool," we are in danger of the judgment of hell. Hell is the judgment of God on all unrighteousness.

We may think we have never done anything *really* bad like murder someone. But Jesus is saying, "When you call someone a slanderous name, you are murdering them. It is the same thing and subject to the same penalty as if you had taken a knife and stuck it through their heart." If we are honest with ourselves, all of us are murderers in this view. All of us so desperately need to be changed, reformed, converted from our murderous ways. If we do not, we are in danger of hellfire, Jesus says.

Therefore, Jesus commands us:

"If you bring your gift to the altar and there remember that your brother has something against you, leave your gift there before the altar, and go your way. First be reconciled to your brother, and then come and offer your gift."
—Matthew 5:23-24

In other words, when you realize you have wronged someone, such as assassinating their character by slanderous name-calling, stop your prayer and your worship of God and make it right with that person first. Humble yourself and do it. Do not think you can go to God and be right with him if you have not done anything to be right with the person you have offended.

Is this not amazing? God is less interested in our worship than he is in our right relationship with each other! God is all about relationship. Jesus is saying our relationship with God is affected if our relationship with others in marred by sin.

How very inconvenient! It blows away all our presumption in worship. It takes away our excuses for why we cannot reconcile with someone. Not only does Jesus inform us of this problem, he gives us the solution: a simple command to go and be reconciled. Lord, help us to obey!

Questions:

1. Think of a time when you "murdered" someone with your words. Did you ever reconcile with that person?

2. Why does Jesus link our relationship with God to our relationship with the people around us?

3. Is Jesus' command to reconcile impossible to obey?

> *"Whoever looks at a woman to lust for her has already committed adultery with her in his heart."*
> —Matthew 5:28

Having addressed the Law against murder, Jesus now turns to the other infamous sin, adultery. He wants us to see we commit this sin not only when we actually sleep with another man's wife, but also when we look at a woman and desire her for ourselves.

Just as he did with murder, Jesus makes it impossible to escape the fact everyone has committed adultery in his heart. He removes all of our excuses and shows us the Law is tied to the attitude of the heart more than the deeds someone could witness. For in the heart, a deed is formed and in the heart it can come to fruition as fantasy just as much as it can ripen into reality.

Jesus demolishes our excuse that pornography really does not hurt anyone. He is saying it hurts *you*. It causes *you* to become adulterous in your mind, even if you do not follow it through, as many do, to become adulterous in action. Besides pornography, however, his statement gives us guidance on how we look at real life people. Do I see them as objects to fulfill my desire? Have they become less than persons and more like commodities?

The implied command in Jesus' statement is: "Do not look lustfully on a woman." It is easier to explain this command away than it is to actually obey it. In fact, to obey this command takes nothing less than the presence and counsel of God's Holy Spirit in a man. Otherwise, we end up arguing about how close to the line we can come without really crossing over.

Questions:

1. How does Jesus' command about adultery change the way you look at people?

2. What excuses have you heard justifying "adultery of the eyes?"

3. Why is Jesus' standard so much higher than the Law's statement, "You shall not commit adultery" (Exodus 20:14)?

"Whoever divorces his wife for any reason except sexual immorality causes her to commit adultery; and whoever marries a woman who is divorced commits adultery."
—Matthew 5:32

"Whoever divorces his wife, except for sexual immorality, and marries another, commits adultery; and whoever marries her who is divorced commits adultery."
—Matthew 19:9

These statements hit very close to home; right at the heart of the home, in fact. Technically, it is not a command. It is Jesus' explanation of the Law's command, "You shall not commit adultery." People who knew the Law, such as the Pharisees, knew the Law included cases where a man would write a certificate of divorce for a wife not pleasing to him. They wondered if a man could divorce his wife for any reason at all:

"Is it lawful for a man to divorce his wife for any and every reason?" (Matthew 19:3)

Again, Jesus smashes our excuses and makes a strong statement in favor of the Law and God's original intention. What he points out is the Law discusses cases where a man may suspect a woman was not a virgin when he married her. If she was not a virgin, he may divorce her, but if this accusation proves to be false, he is forbidden from divorcing her ever (Deuteronomy 22:13-19).

In referencing divorce, the Law considers it in cases where the man finds something "indecent" about his wife, such as the fact she was not a virgin when he married her. Jesus reinforces this by saying, "Whoever divorces his wife for any reason *except sexual immorality*, and marries another, commits adultery."

The purpose of the Law was to acknowledge there are cases of sexual immorality where one marriage partner violates the marriage covenant. In such cases, it simply recognizes the fact the deceived marriage partner may want to divorce based on the deception inherent in the marriage. Because marriage is a promise and a gift of God, a deceptive marriage is really not marriage. It is based on a lie rather than a promise. The Law recognized this and acknowledged the right of the deceived person to divorce.

The natural human tendency, however, is to take this as a license to divorce for any reason we choose. This is seen in the Pharisee question to Jesus of Matthew 19:3. Jesus does not reformulate the Law, he simply restates it more explicitly. Unless sexual immorality is involved, thus making the marriage no marriage at all, but a deception, it is adulterous to marry another.

We always want to find excuses and exceptions. Jesus gives us none except the one already present in the Law. He does more than that, however. He also explains *why* the Law says it.

"What God has joined together, let not man separate."
—Matthew 19:6

Marriage is a joining together of a man and woman performed by God. It is what he did for Adam and Eve in the beginning. It is not a ceremony, but a state of life. In fact, the Bible never records a ceremony for Adam and Eve, yet Genesis calls her Adam's "wife" (Genesis 2:25). In fact, Jesus quotes the previous verse (Genesis 2:24) when he says, "For this reason a man will leave his father and mother and be united to his wife, and the two will become one flesh." (Matthew 19:5)

The point is, God has joined a man and his wife together. We should never separate what God has joined unless the separation occurred by the deceptive sexual immorality of one of the parties. In this case, the deceptive person is the one who has separated the two by joining themselves with another.

Jesus leaves no "wiggle room" for us to squeeze out of the fact we must work through our relationships in life and not run away from them for just any reason. In fact, he acknowledges only one reason, the one acknowledged by God in the Law. If we are to obey Jesus, we must deny all of our excuses, exceptions, and special cases. Or, as Jesus responds to his disciples when they are shocked by this teaching,

> *"He who is able to accept it, let him accept it."*
> —Matthew 19:12

The command is this: "Accept it."

Questions:

1. Can you accept Jesus' teaching about divorce and re-marriage?

2. If you have made a mistake in the past regarding this issue, are you willing to acknowledge it to God and ask for his forgiveness and the forgiveness of the people affected?

3. Why would God be so concerned about sexual behavior between humans?

4. Do you find yourself looking for exceptions or ready to obey Jesus in this matter, regardless of the personal cost?

> *"Do not swear at all: neither by heaven, for it is God's throne; nor by the earth, for it is His footstool; nor by Jerusalem, for it is the city of the great King. Neither shall you swear by your head, because you cannot make one hair white or black. But let your 'Yes' be 'Yes' and your 'No,' 'No'. Anything beyond this comes from the evil one."*
> —Matthew 5:34-37

Why would Jesus care about taking an oath? Perhaps it has something to do with what an oath really is. People take an oath to establish credibility. In court, you are required to swear or affirm on the Bible because no one involved really knows you enough to establish if you are trustworthy. By appealing to something which used to be highly esteemed in our popular culture (God's Word), swearing shows a seriousness about what you are saying in a situation: you are not just telling your stories or opinions to a friend over dinner. There can be no "fish tales" or exaggerations, only the straight and simple truth as you know it.

Jesus is encouraging us to be truthful people all of the time. He says making any kind of embellishment upon your "yes" or "no" answer is Satan's way. It is the liar who needs to establish credibility where there is none. Only a deceiver must appeal to something outside themselves for truth. A truthful person has the truth inside and requires no enhancement to their confidence in the truth.

By appealing to the credibility of the thing or person outside yourself, you are appropriating the respect owed to that thing or person for yourself. You are stealing their reputation. So if I swear an oath by heaven, Jesus says I am using the authority of God's throne to buttress my own authority. Swearing by the earth is using his footstool for the same purpose. When I swear by my own head, even this is not really my own; God is the one who made me. Do not steal God's authority and use it to establish your own credibility. Instead, have the truth in you and you will not need anything else.

Questions:

1. Have you ever tried to bolster someone's confidence in what you say by using the reputation or authority of something or someone outside yourself?

2. Why does Jesus say anything beyond simple truthfulness "comes from the evil one?" Why is it Satan's tactic?

3. How can you establish credibility without taking oaths?

"I tell you not to resist an evil person. But whoever slaps you on your right cheek, turn the other to him also....Give to him who asks you, and from him who wants to borrow from you do not turn away."

—Matthew 5:39, 42

When we read this command, it is easy to think Jesus has completely no concept of life in the real world. Do not resist an evil person? If no one ever resisted evil, there would be no good people left in the world! It helps to remember Jesus is systematically explaining the meaning of the Law to his disciples piece by piece in this section of the Gospel of Matthew. Previously, he discussed his stand on murder, adultery, divorce, and oath-taking.

This is the Law he explains with this statement, "You have heard it said, 'Eye for eye and tooth for tooth.'" (Matthew 5:38) The Law gave guidelines on how far vengeance could go. It kept a dispute from escalating into an arms race. One could extract no more vengeance than the wrong done.

What Jesus adds by way of explanation is even though the Law says you have the right to extract an eye for vengeance if an eye was taken, do not resist the person who has wronged you. If they insult you (strike you on the cheek) or sue you to take away your possessions, offer them more. "Give to him who asks you." No conditions.

Why would Jesus make this statement? In every conflict, there must be someone who initiates the end of the matter by making peace, even if they have to give up the right to have the last word. He has already made it clear the sons of God are peacemakers (Matthew 5:9). The peacemaker is the one who will suffer loss in order to buy peace. There is nothing in this world worth more than ending a conflict with another person except human life. If humans are eternal (Jesus says they are, John 3:36) and material things are not (Jesus says they are not, Matthew 6:19), then it is a small price to pay a material thing to restore a human relationship. Even injury to one's own pride is a small price to pay.

Seen from an eternal perspective, it is we who rarely have a concept of life in the real world, the world including eternity. Jesus helps us see this world and the fullness of the Law.

Questions:

1. Is Jesus telling us to be pacifists?

2. What do we gain by suffering material loss in a conflict?

3. How can we allow ourselves to be insulted and not speak up in our own defense? Why should we?

4. What is Jesus' fuller picture of reality?

"Love your enemies, bless those who curse you, do good to those who hate you, and pray for those who spitefully use you and persecute you....Be perfect, therefore, as your heavenly Father is perfect."

—Matthew 5:44,48

If we were tempted to think Jesus was out of touch with reality when he told us not to resist an evil person, we are completely shocked by the command to love our enemies, to actively care about their well-being. Who is an enemy except someone who is actively working against our own best interests? If our enemies work against us, why should we work for their good? Does this not assist them in working against us?

Jesus gives us an objective standard. He says to "bless" them, "do good" to them, and to "pray" for them. Each of these are tied to what God does for us. He has blessed us with life and continual provision to sustain life. "He causes his sun to rise on the evil and the good, and sends rain on the righteous and the unrighteous." (Matthew 5:45) To bless our enemies, we would acknowledge their right to exist and protect that right, actively promoting their existence, just as God promotes ours.

Doing good to our enemies is also an objective standard. It is what God does for all. Even when God brings judgment and wrath, it is for the purpose of bringing about repentance. "He is patient with you, not wanting anyone to perish, but everyone to come to repentance." (2 Peter 3:9) Likewise, when we must confront an enemy, our motive for the confrontation should be the enemy's greater good, not their destruction. For example, if someone murders a family member, I do not go buy a gun and kill them in return. Instead, I call the police and get the lawful authorities to arrest them. How can this be doing them good?

My motive is not to kill them in vengeance. Instead, they must face the righteous requirements of the law. Perhaps they will turn from their ways in prison, realizing they have lived a life of sin and need God's forgiveness as well as mine?

How can we pray for our enemies? If we truly seek to obey Jesus' command, we must actively seek their good before God and ask it for them. Many times, our enemies do not know God and would be unable to ask him themselves. At the least, we have Jesus' own example of praying for those who nailed him to the cross: "Father, forgive them, for they do not know what they are doing." (Luke 23:34) As a minimum, we can ask God to forgive our enemies their sins against us, with which we are very familiar.

Perhaps the greatest thrust of Jesus' command to love our enemies is not in what we do for them, but what our obedience to this command does for us. By taking on God's way of blessing both the righteous and unrighteous, seeking the good of even an evil person, and praying for them, we are displaying God's character in ourselves. We are becoming more like God. Or, as Jesus said, "that you may be sons of your Father in heaven." (Matthew 5:45)

Having his character in us is the only way we could ever hope to "be perfect" as our Father is perfect.

Questions.

1. Is Jesus asking too much for us to love our enemies?

2. What are the three things Jesus tells us to do for our enemies?

3. Who is your enemy?

4. What is the purpose of obeying this command?

"Do not do your charitable deeds before men, to be seen by them."

—Matthew 6:1

Much charitable activity is not really charity because it is done for selfish reasons, such as to enhance one's reputation. For a deed to be charitable, Jesus is saying it must be done for real charity or pure love. You must not do it in order to gain something else.

In fact, the ultimate charitable deed is to die for another person. You stand to gain nothing by dying. It is also the model Jesus gave us: "While we were yet sinners, Christ died for us." (Romans 5:8).

The Bible has many promises about how we will be blessed if we care for the poor, widows, and orphans. For example, "He who gives to the poor will lack nothing." (Proverbs 28:27) This is not the reason, however, we help them. We do so out of love for them, compassion for their circumstances, a desire to make right whatever we can in their relationship with God and man. Is this not what Jesus really came to do? He healed the sick, making their bodies whole. He preached the gospel, encouraging them to wholeness with God. The incredible thing is he did it all for love. There were no entrance fees, no offerings taken, not even an obligation laid on the people to do as he said.

This is the real thing: charity. It cannot be faked because it has no other agenda. It stands to lose much but continues to operate. It is the very character and power of God. In fact, the Bible says "Love never fails." (1 Corinthians 13:8) It continues for eternity and it always accomplishes its purpose: to love the other. Is this not amazing? No one can stop you from loving another person! They may be able to kill your body, but they cannot stop you from loving. This is a deep mystery to be meditated upon.

In loving, let us make sure our motives are correct as Jesus tells us. Jesus takes it one step farther, however, and addresses our motivations even in prayer.

> *"When you pray, you shall not be like the hypocrites. For they love to pray standing in the synagogues and on the corners of the streets, that they may be seen by men....But you, when you pray, go into your room, and when you have shut the door, pray to your Father who is in the secret place; and your Father who sees in secret will reward you openly."*
> —Matthew 6:5-6

> *"When you fast, do not be like the hypocrites, with a sad countenance....But you, when you fast, anoint your head and wash your face, so that you do not appear to men to be fasting."*
> —Matthew 6:17-18

In the matter of our deeds, Jesus has already addressed our motivations and insisted they must be pure for the deed to have eternal value. Now, in these commands, he has turned to prayer. When we pray or fast, he insists it must not be done in order to be seen by others.

In churches and Christian organizations, this can be a real temptation. Prayer meetings can turn into a "see and be seen" kind of social gathering. Again, Jesus comes back to the motive of the heart. If you would not close your door and pray to your Father, then do not go out in public and do so. God hears the cry of your heart and is not impressed by your public performance.

Jesus is also making a statement about God in this command. Our Father hears our prayers even from the secret place, where no one else knows and often no one cares. Not only does he hear those prayers and comfort us privately, he will reward us openly as Jesus says. If we wish to be exalted publicly, we must first encounter God privately. If we need to be vindicated before men, first engage with God. It is a statement of priority in relationships: God first, others after. In this way, our social relationships will have proper perspective and balance. Without God first, they become distorted by our concern about how others feel about us.

Questions:

1. Should we be afraid if someone notices us doing a charitable deed?

2. Why can we not fake real love?

3. What is our reward for charitable deeds?

4. Should we never pray publicly?

5. How does Jesus' command regarding prayer establish priorities in our relationships?

"When you pray, do not use vain repetitions as the heathen do. For they think that they will be heard for their many words."

—Matthew 6:7

Jesus is telling his disciples how to pray. His first command, after he has addressed the issue of having a private relationship with God, is not to use "vain repetitions." Who are the people who exhibit this behavior? The "heathen," or unbelievers do this because their gods are projections of their own imaginations upon reality. They pray to their idols or concepts of the Divine. Because of this, they repeat themselves in prayer. There is really no one there to address. Instead, they are subconsciously trying to convince themselves they will get that for which they ask.

Prayer is not the power of positive thinking. It is a conversation with the one who created and sustains us. God *is* and he cares. The way we pray can be a statement of our faith in God. Do we really believe he is there? Do we believe he really cares? If so, then we need not repeat ourselves in prayer to him.

In fact, it is *we* who must begin to understand, not God. We are the ones who enter prayer with an incomplete picture of reality. We need God to explain things to us, not the other way around!

Jesus gives us his vision of prayer in the following verses:

"Our Father in heaven, hallowed be your name, your kingdom come, your will be done on earth as it is in heaven. Give us today our daily bread. Forgive us our debts, as we also have forgiven our debtors. And lead us not into temptation, but deliver us from the evil one."

—Matthew 6:9-13

> "When you pray, say: Our Father in heaven, hallowed be your name. Your kingdom come. Your will be done on earth as it is in heaven. Give us day by day our daily bread. And forgive us our sins, for we also forgive anyone who is indebted to us. And do not lead us into temptation, but deliver us from the evil one."
>
> —Luke 11:2-4

Much of the prayer focuses on God rather than yourself, on his will and its accomplishment in the world. It acknowledges our need for God's provision and forgiveness, as well as asks him to keep us from testing. In Jesus' prayer, we see our need to be delivered from the power of Satan. Without relationship with God, we are doomed to take life as it comes to us and it can come very hard, full of trials, tests, and evil deceit.

If we take Jesus and his attitude in prayer seriously, we see we are putting ourselves on the line with God to forgive others.

> "For if you forgive men their trespasses, your heavenly Father will also forgive you. But if you do not forgive men their trespasses, neither will your Father forgive your trespasses."
>
> —Matthew 6:14-15

We are committing ourselves to follow God in forgiveness because we are asking for the same treatment from God as we give to others. It is a different way of thinking about the world. In relationship with God, we can proactively change the world by changing *our* attitudes. We no longer are locked into responding to the trials, tests, and deceit in kind. Instead, we can now trust God, endure, and forgive. The way we pray impacts the way we live.

Questions:

1. What is prayer?

2. How does repetition in prayer display a lack of faith in God?

3. How does prayer change the way we live?

> *"Do not lay up for yourselves treasures on earth, where moth and rust destroy and thieves break in and steal; but lay up for yourselves treasures in heaven"*
> —Matthew 6:19-20

Jesus gives us his investment strategy for wealth creation. Unlike an investment advisor, however, he is not merely a consultant. Instead, he is our Lord commanding us how to use what he has given us in this life. Specifically, Jesus is talking about money.

This can be seen by the context of the surrounding verses, most importantly Matthew 6:24, "No one can serve two masters. Either he will hate the one and love the other, or he will be devoted to the one and despise the other. You cannot serve both God and Money."

In Matthew 6:19-20, it is not so clear how to attain the heavenly treasures, only that you should invest this way. Jesus makes it clearer in another command found in Matthew 19:21. Here he is speaking to a rich young man who asks how he can attain eternal life.

> *"If you want to enter into life, keep the commandments.... You shall not murder, you shall not commit adultery, you shall not steal, you shall not bear false witness, honor your father and mother, and you shall love your neighbor as yourself....If you want to be perfect, go sell what you have and give to the poor, and you will have treasure in heaven; and come, follow Me."*
> —Matthew 19:17-21

The two commands are related. In the first, Jesus tells us to lay up treasures in heaven. In the second, he tells us how to do this. It is not enough to simply follow the commandments of God or think you are doing so. The rich young man said, "All these things I have kept." (Matthew 19:21) Jesus appreciated the man's desire to please God by following the commandments. In Mark's Gospel, we discover "Jesus looked at him and loved him." (Mark 10:21) He appreciated the young man's heart attitude. Regarding eternal life, however, Jesus informed him he needed to "follow me" if he wanted to pursue the one thing he still lacked. Without Jesus, we cannot have eternal life.

The command about investing our money is an aside, a parenthetical statement in Jesus' response to this man about eternal life. Yet it has bearing on the young man's question as well. For if we attain eternal life, what *kind* of life will it be? What will be our "quality of life?" The amount of "treasure in heaven" could determine this.

If we think clearly about the matter, we can begin to see Jesus' point and why he would tie eternal life and heavenly treasure together. The kind of life we live eternally cannot depend on our earthly treasures. We do not take them with us into that age. One thing we do retain, however, is our character. We know we shall be changed in body, yet still the same person. Paul states as much in 1 Corinthians 15:50-51, "I declare to you, brothers, that flesh and blood cannot inherit the kingdom of God, nor does the perishable inherit the imperishable. Listen, I tell you a mystery: we will not all sleep, but we will all be changed."

Our essential personhood, our character, *who we are*, does not change, however. This is what will be judged by God in the Last Day. A picture of this can be seen in Revelation 20:11-12, *"Then I saw a great white throne and him who was seated on it. Earth and sky fled from his presence, and there was no place for them. And I saw the dead, great and small, standing before the throne, and books were opened. Another book was opened, which is the book of life. The dead were judged according to what they had done as recorded in the books."*

Those who do not believe the Gospel are not found in the book of life. This is why Jesus encourages the rich young man to follow him beyond simply trying to obey the commandments. But the judgment of believers also takes place based on what is written in the book of life. Even believers will be judged by what they have done as recorded in this book.

What you do reflects your character, who you really are. We can say one thing and do another, but think about what you would call a "good person." It is someone who consistently does good as well as speaks it. These kinds of people stand out in the world because their character matches their rhetoric.

In effect, Jesus is saying, "Look, if you want God to be your master, then here is how you should spend your money. Here is how I want you to create wealth: give your money to the poor. Your treasure will be in heaven."

There is a guaranteed return-on-investment with Jesus' strategy. He says what will happen: you *will* have treasure in heaven. This does not seem so strange at all when we realize by giving to the poor, we are developing a *generous* character, which is exactly one of the character traits our God so abundantly displays. Actually, we can begin to see the pay-off of godly character even in this life. Even if we do not, however, it is eternally secure in the Bank of Heaven, guaranteed by God no one can take it away from us. Money seems a very poor investment compared to this!

Questions:

1. What is Jesus' command to us about money?

2. How do we gain eternal riches?

3. What kind of life do you want to live forever?

4. What form could our "treasure in heaven" take that we might even notice now?

"Do not worry about your life, what you will eat or what you will drink; nor about your body, what you will put on. Is not life more than food and the body more than clothing?"
—Matthew 6:25

"Do not worry about your life, what you will eat; nor about the body, what you will put on. Life is more than food and the body is more than clothing. Consider the ravens, for they neither sow nor reap, which have neither storehouse nor barn; and God feeds them. Of how much more value are you than birds?....And do not seek what you should eat or what you should drink, nor have an anxious mind....But seek the kingdom of God, and all these thing shall be added to you."
—Luke 12:22-24,29,31

"Do not fear, little flock, for it is your Father's good pleasure to give you the kingdom. Sell what you have and give alms; provide yourselves money bags which do not grow old, a treasure in the heavens that does not fail, where no thief approaches nor moth destroys."
Luke 12:32 34

Having spoken to us about how to spend our money to attain heavenly treasures, Jesus returns to answer the obvious objections. "But how will I live? How can I provide for myself and my family if I give my money to the poor?" These questions are in everyone's mind when we begin to take Jesus' command about money seriously.

It is worthwhile to notice Jesus did not say, "Quit your job and give everything to the poor." Instead, he encouraged us **not** to "lay up for yourselves treasures on earth." In certain cases, Jesus may call us to quit our job, such as the rich young man, whom he also offered the job of a lifetime: to follow him and participate in his earthly ministry as a disciple. Jesus also did not say to deny yourself everything in a superhuman effort of asceticism.

Instead, Jesus simply tells us not to worry about our lives. If we give money to the poor and we have less than we thought we needed for living, he assures us God will provide for us what we need. Besides, "is not life more than food and the body more than clothing?" There is more to life than these things, although life does consist of these things in part.

Jesus commands us to seek the kingdom of God, not a new car or other possessions. All the things we need for life will be provided by God if we trust him enough to live our lives with his priorities. We need not worry.

Clearly, Jesus is not talking about being lazy and waiting for everything to fall in your lap. He uses the analogy of the ravens to show what our lives should be like. They search for food and work hard at it all day; God provides it for them. They, however, do not worry about getting their food, they simply go about the business of living. Jesus is commanding us to live for God's kingdom, go about our business, knowing God will take care of what we need. It is the worry and fear we can do without.

Jesus is telling us something about God here also. "It is your Father's good pleasure to give you the kingdom." He *wants* to give us everything he has! In fact, God wants to give us *more* than what our minds are even capable of wanting. He wants to give us his very character, a possession of priceless value. No one can ever take this treasure away.

Questions:

1. How can worry keep us from seeking the kingdom of God?

2. What does this command tell us about God?

3. Is God asking you to leave your job? If so, what other job does he have for you to do?

4. Do we need to work?

"Seek first the kingdom of God and his righteousness, and all these things shall be added to you."
—Matthew 6:33

"Do not worry about tomorrow, for tomorrow will worry about its own things."
—Matthew 6:34

God wants to give us even more than his character. Eternal life begins *now*, right here on earth, when we begin to follow Jesus. It is not reserved only for after death. It is not a stage of life, but a new life altogether. Eternal life has different priorities than our former life.

Paul says, "Put to death, therefore, whatever belongs to your earthly nature: sexual immorality, impurity, lust, evil desires and greed, which is idolatry. Because of these, the wrath of God is coming. You used to walk in these ways, in the life you once lived. But now you must rid yourselves of all such things as these." (Colossians 3:5-8)

What is it then in this new life we should want? How do we "seek the kingdom of God and his righteousness?"

Later in the same scripture, Paul gives us examples of what we should be seeking. "Therefore, as God's chosen people, holy and dearly loved, clothe yourselves with compassion, kindness, humility, gentleness, and patience. Bear with each other and forgive whatever grievances you may have against one another. Forgive as the Lord forgave you. And over all these virtues put on love, which binds them all together in perfect unity." (Colossians 3:12-14)

Each of these is a character trait of God. These are the "treasures in heaven" Jesus wishes us to accumulate. They are, however, to be worked out here, not in heaven. We have our opportunity to exercise them now and fully possess them in the resurrection age to come.

Jesus says if we seek these things, then all of our needs such as food and clothing will be given to us as well. God will give us what we need; we can trust him. The whole command centers around this trust, not only for today, but our whole lives. Do we trust God with our future as well as our present? Jesus says we can and should.

In fact, Jesus specifically commands us not to worry about tomorrow. Our tomorrow is a part of the Eternal Today if we are living eternal life. We can even see this in the name God calls himself to Moses when asked by what name God should be called.

"This is what you are to say to the Israelites: 'I AM has sent me to you.'" God is eternally *present* in the past, future, all of life. This eternal life is what we are entering into with Jesus. To worry about tomorrow is to not completely apprehend this magnificent gift. We are eternal people in Jesus, the Christ. There is nothing to fear in the future.

Questions:

1. What is the "kingdom of God?"

2. How do we experience his kingdom now?

3. Does how we worry about material things say something about our trust in God?

4. How does our view of the future say something about our trust in God?

5. What could be meant by the term "Eternal Today?"

"Judge not, that you not be judged. For with the judgment you judge, you will be judged; and with the measure you use, it will be measured back to you."
—Matthew 7:1-2

"Judge not, and you shall not be judged. Condemn not, and you shall not be condemned. Forgive, and you will be forgiven. Give, and it will be given to you: good measure, pressed down, shaken together, and running over will be put into your bosom. For with the same measure you use, it will be measured back to you."
—Luke 6:37-38

Jesus commands us not to judge others. To judge another person is to look at them with what you see and claim to know what is in their heart. Judgment depends on our human reason and is therefore flawed. It can be very wrong; but even if our human judgment is correct, there is danger for us in judging others.

The danger lies in the fact that judgment has consequences. If I judge the heart of another, I then believe I am justified in treating someone a certain way. I believe this because I think I know what they are about and what they deserve. God knows what everyone deserves, even me. By judging another, I come in danger of judgment myself because the Lord has been very gracious in forgiving my sins, faults, mistakes, and even my knowingly wicked acts.

Jesus told a parable about a servant who owed his master a large sum of money (Matthew 18:23-35). The master forgave the debt when the servant pleaded with him, but the servant did not forgive a fellow servant the small debt he owed. When the master learned of this, he gave the unforgiving servant over to the torturers and prison. Jesus' point is we are required by God to display the same kind of mercy he has shown to us.

In fact, Jesus told this parable in response to his disciple Peter's question as to how many times he would have to forgive someone who offends him. Jesus responded,

> *"I do not say to you, up to seven times, but up to seventy times seven."*
>
> —Matthew 18:22

In other words, show the kind of unending mercy God has shown towards you.

Judging another prevents us from obeying this command. It also blocks our ability to let go of an offense and truly forgive from the heart. Instead, it gives us a justification for why we can continue to be angry with someone and perhaps think they can never change because "that's the kind of person they are." This is the most dangerous kind of judgment, for you can be sure you are well on your way to the torturers like the unforgiving servant if you nurse such an attitude.

It is tempting to explain away this command of Jesus theologically because its ramifications are uncomfortable. The simple fact remains, however, *all* of us are tempted to judge others and Jesus is warning us we receive from God the same standard of judgment we use on others. It is our choice which one he will use on us: strict or lenient.

Questions:

1. What is "judging" another?

2. Why are we all tempted to judge others with a stricter judgment than we use for ourselves?

3. How does God judge us?

4. How will our attitude in forgiving others determine our own judgment by God?

"First remove the plank from your own eye, and then you will see clearly to remove the speck from your brother's eye."
—Matthew 7:5

"First remove the plank from your own eye, and then you will see clearly to remove the speck that is in your brother's eye."
—Luke 6:42

"Do not judge according to appearance, but judge with righteous judgment."
—John 7:24

"He who is without sin among you, let him throw a stone at her first."
—John 8:7

"Go and sin no more."
—John 8:11

While Jesus has commanded us not to judge, he has not ordered us to have lobotomies. This command to remove the plank before removing another's speck is an example of the *realness* of Jesus. He knows we will encounter people and situations where we notice wrongdoing in others. It is inevitable.

The interesting aspect of his approach to this is he does not order us to ignore the faults of others. He has told us not to judge in order to avoid harsh judgment ourselves, but he also instructs us how to deal with the reality of sin in other people. First, we are to be mindful of our own sin. We must confess or "own up to" the sin in our own lives before we are qualified to address the sin in others. This simple first step can eliminate so much conflict because it has to do with adjusting our attitude.

When we approach another, mindful of our own sin and need of forgiveness, we are much more likely to come humbly and without offense. We do not come with a pointed finger and accusations (which is the definition of "Satan", as "Satan" means "accuser"). Instead, we will come in love, stating the facts and concerned about the well-being of the person and others affected by the sin.

Secondly, we must "<u>see clearly</u> to remove the speck from your brother's eye." Often, we do not understand the circumstances of a situation we think we see. We confront someone and realize there was more to the story than we thought. Confessing our own sin is a first step, as it makes our attitude one sensitive enough to see clearly what reality is in this situation. God will show us what we need to see in order to bring healing and reconciliation to sinful situations. He wants this even more than we do! But he is not willing to resort to accusation and condemnation in order to achieve righteousness.

Paul wrote, "But now a righteousness from God, apart from law, has been made known, to which the Law and the Prophets testify. This righteousness from God comes through faith in Jesus Christ to all who believe." (Romans 3:21-22)

When confronted with the wrongdoing of another, it is also helpful to remember our righteousness does not come from our obedience to the Law. It comes from God, through faith in Christ. So if we are right and another is wrong, it is not because we are a better person. Rather, it is the grace of God in this situation which gives me the ability to clearly see the fault. I must not be arrogant or proud because this grace was given to me for a reason: their benefit. God is allowing me to be a part of reconciling them to himself in this particular situation.

If anyone was justified in condemning someone, it was Jesus. The Bible tells us he was without sin (Hebrews 4:15). When he encountered a woman caught in the very act of adultery, Jesus displayed for us his attitude towards sinners (John 8:3-11).

First, he addressed the Pharisees and teachers of the Law who brought the woman to him, "If any one of you is without sin, let him be the first to throw a stone at her." (John 8:7) Second, he addressed the woman, "Has no one condemned you?"

"No one, sir," she said.

"Then neither do I condemn you," Jesus declared. "Go now and leave your life of sin." (John 8:10-11)

His first step was to help the Pharisees and scribes realize their own sinfulness before addressing the sin of another. Secondly, he addressed the sinner with compassion and encouraged her to leave the sin behind. The reconciliation of the sinner was his goal, not her condemnation.

Jesus gave us a wonderful example of how to take the plank out of our own eye before pulling the speck out of another's. If we follow his command and example, our confrontations will be less intimidating and offensive, while actually accomplishing what he wants: reconciliation of sinners.

Questions:

1. Does Jesus want us to ignore the sins of others?

2. How do we approach another's sinfulness?

3. Where does righteousness come from and how do we attain it?

4. What is "seeing clearly" to "pull the speck out" of someone else's eye?

"Do not give what is holy to the dogs; nor cast your pearls before swine, lest they trample them under their feet, and turn and tear you to pieces."
—Matthew 7:6

This is a very curious command. It seems to have nothing to do with the context of the scripture around it. However, Jesus has just commanded us not to judge others but rather to "see clearly" in addressing their sin. He does not want us to ignore the sin of others. The words Jesus speaks to us are holy pearls, our most precious possessions. "Let the word of Christ dwell in you richly as you teach and admonish one another with all wisdom," Paul writes to the Colossians. They are priceless and eternal: "Heaven and earth will pass away, but my words will never pass away." (Matthew 24:35)

Now, when we see others clearly, fully aware of our own sin, there will be times when we see another person does not want to hear the word of God. They have a hard heart, unwilling to listen to what Jesus has said. In this case, Jesus is telling us not to "cast our pearls," the precious word God has revealed to us, on these people at this particular time. They do not want to hear. In fact, they will react violently to hearing the words of Jesus.

The Proverbs tell the same truth, "A mocker resents correction; he will not consult the wise." (Proverbs 15:12) The thread of this idea runs throughout the Proverbs in several places:

"The fear of the Lord is the beginning of knowledge, but fools despise wisdom and discipline." (Proverbs 1:7)

"A longing fulfilled is sweet to the soul, but a fool detests turning from evil." (Proverbs 13:19)

"Fools mock at making amends for sin, but goodwill is found among the upright." (Proverbs 14:9)

So Jesus is not giving a new command, he is merely telling us what God has already taught through Solomon's proverbs. The point is not that we should never preach the word of God to a fool. If this were the case, we would never preach to anyone who needs to hear it! What Jesus is saying is to hold back the sensitive, delicate, personal experience of God from such a person. They will not be able to respond to a personal experience of God until their heart has been softened by the Holy Spirit to receive the Gospel first.

In the Parable of the Sower, Jesus told of a person who heard the word of God, but did not believe. "A farmer went out to sow his seed. As he was scattering the seed, some fell along the path, and the birds came and ate it up....When anyone hears the message about the kingdom and does not understand it, the evil one comes and snatches away what was sown in his heart." (Matthew 13:3-4, 19) A hardened heart is unable to understand the mysteries of God. In fact, exposure to the mysteries of God can cause a violent reaction in such a person. Keep your personal encounters of God's deeper workings to yourself when you are dealing with a hardened heart. The Bible gives a good example of what a hard heart looks like.

"But the Lord hardened Pharaoh's heart, and he would not let them go. Pharaoh said to Moses, 'Get out of my sight! Make sure you do not appear before me again! The day you see my face you will die.'

'Just as you say,' Moses replied, 'I will never appear before you again.'" (Exodus 10:27-29)

Pharaoh reacted so violently to God's word spoken through Moses that he threatened to kill Moses. Do you think it would have been wise for Moses to continue to attempt to convince Pharaoh of his folly by explaining how God had shown himself so faithful to Moses in the past? Would it have changed Pharaoh's mind if Moses had talked with Pharaoh about his personal testimony and how graciously God had treated him?

Absolutely not! This is what Jesus was referring to when he said not to "cast your pearls before swine, lest they trample them under their feet, and turn and tear you to pieces."

Questions:

1. What does a "hard heart" look like?

2. What is a "pearl" in Jesus' command?

3. Why would Jesus command us to withhold our "pearls" from a hard-hearted person?

4. Why would we want to avoid the violent reaction of a hardened heart to the mysteries of God?

"Ask and it will be given to you; seek, and you will find; knock, and it will be opened to you."
—Matthew 7:7

"I say to you, ask and it will be given to you; seek, and you will find; knock, and it will be opened to you."
—Luke 11:9

Jesus tells us to ask God for what we want, seek him, knock on his door for answers. This is more than a command to seek God for the things we want. It is a statement about God himself and our relationship with him. If we are unwilling to ask God for those things we desire, we are holding part of our lives back from him. In fact, we are holding the most important part of our lives back. For what is more important to us than the things about which we dream?

Jesus commands us to cut God in on our dreams, not because God is unaware of them, but because he is the source of their fulfillment. We may attain a goal in many ways, but we will not see the true desire of our hearts fulfilled unless we involve God in the process. Why is this?

What Jesus is saying about God is he will give to us, he will help us find what we are looking for, he will open the doors closed to us. In fact, he will do more than this. He will open the *right* doors. He will give us what will truly fulfill us rather than what will simply fill us up. He *wants* to do this.

In the history of religion, no one has ever made such a statement about any god. There has never been a case where a god is portrayed as *wanting* to fulfill human dreams. At times, pagan gods and goddesses are portrayed as having favorite humans they shower favor upon, but it was always for their own inscrutable purposes. In this case, Jesus is saying God thinks of us as being in a Father-son relationship with him. As our Father, he wants to provide what he can to fulfill our dreams. These verses immediately follow Jesus' command:

"For everyone who asks, receives; he who seeks finds; and to him who knocks, the door will be opened. Which of you, if his son asks for bread, will give him a stone? Or if he asks for a fish, will give him a snake? If you, then, though you are evil know how to give good gifts to your children, how much more will your Father in heaven give good gifts to those who ask him!" (Matthew 7:8-11)

In Luke's Gospel, the last verse reads just a bit differently, but gives a fuller sense of what Jesus is talking about.

"If you, then, who are evil, know how to give good gifts to your children, how much more will your Father in heaven give the Holy Spirit to those who ask him?" (Luke 11:13)

The "good gifts" God gives us are not just the trifling things we so often want for ourselves. Why bother with a Porsche sports car when you can have the Holy Spirit? In eternity, you will have infinitely more horsepower with the Holy Spirit than with a rusty old Porsche, even though it started out sparkling new when you got it. The Holy Spirit is God himself, his Spirit. All our dreams and aspirations find their fulfillment in God and he is very willing to give us of himself!

This may seem to be evading the point. When you ask for a Porsche, you want a sports car, not God. Think, why do you want the sports car? Is it the speed, power, prestige? Is it because it is one of the best cars in the world, excellent in every way? All of these things are qualities of God; the Porsche only has them in a small way compared with him. At the deeper level, we desire things because they imitate God in some way, a way appealing to us. So both Matthew's and Luke's accounts are correct. The Father will give us good gifts, especially the Holy Spirit, the greatest gift of all.

Questions:

1. Why will we not receive the true desire of our heart unless God gives it to us?

2. What does this command say about God?

3. How could the Holy Spirit encompass every good gift we can imagine?

> *"Whatever you want men to do to you, do also to them, for this is the Law and the Prophets."*
> —Matthew 7:12

Here is Jesus' Golden Rule, yet it could also be called the Golden Command. Indeed, he says it is a summary of all of the teaching of the Law and Prophets, every command given by God to men. Curiously enough, Jesus does not point us to God directly or to God's commands as measuring sticks for our proper behavior. He gives us an *internal* measuring stick, one with us all the time, in every situation of life: picture yourself as the other person. How would *you* want to be treated?

We are very good at excusing ourselves because we know why we feel or do certain things. In effect, we are very *forgiving* of ourselves. If we applied the Golden Command, then, we would be forgiving of others, try to understand their situations, and apply grace to their shortcomings. Usually, however, we find it easy to find the faults in others and use those faults to excuse our own behavior. This produces exactly the opposite effect of what Jesus wants. We need to use the faults of others to overlook their annoying behaviors.

Everyone expects to be shown some basic *respect*. They do not expect to be ignored or treated as having no value. This is based on the fact God has created us. What God created has value in and of itself, regardless of its utility. A tree has value simply because it is a creation of God, not only because I can chop it into firewood. How much more then, does a human being have intrinsic value? Every person deserves our respect out of respect for their Creator. How would a potter feel if we went through his workshop and smashed each piece of pottery he had created? He would be very angry! Treating his handiwork with such contempt would show disrespect for the potter. So it is with God. Since we expect to be treated as having value, Jesus is simply commanding us to apply this fact to all other people in how we treat them.

A third aspect of this internal measuring stick is *benevolence*. We want others to have good intentions toward us. We do not want people to be actively working against us. While this does not actually require others to help us, we would at least like people to not hinder our efforts in life. Still, we would like others to help us as much as they are able. Doesn't it make you feel good when someone is at least cheering for you? They may not be able to come on the playing field and help you win the game, but you know they want you to win. A benevolent attitude lets others know you want them to win in life. You may not be able to actively assist in every circumstance, but benevolence lets them know you are **for** them.

Questions:

1. Why would Jesus give us an internal measuring stick against which to measure our attitudes and actions towards others?

2. How does this internal measure work with the external measure of God's Word revealed to us in the Bible?

3. Are there other attitudes you expect from others towards yourself besides forgiveness, respect, and benevolence?

> *"Enter by the narrow gate; for wide is the gate and broad is the way that leads to destruction, and there are many who go by it."*
> —Matthew 7:13

One thing is clear about this Captain Jesus. He is not interested in winning popularity contests or making people feel comfortable. He is always encouraging us to go farther, to take the hard way, "the one less traveled" in the words of American poet Robert Frost. The easy and popular way, the paved road, so to speak, lies on the way to destruction. It involves no effort, difficulty, struggle, or pain. There will be many to accompany you on this road.

The next verse tells us the gate and road leading to life are small and narrow. In fact, Jesus goes so far as to say "only a few find it." There must be something about the kind of life Jesus is discussing which is unattractive and generally unpopular. The destination of each road must be somewhat obscured to the travelers or else no one would travel the broad path to destruction. The life at the end of the narrow road is obscured by the difficulty of the path and miniscule size of the gate.

How discouraging!

Perhaps this is exactly Jesus' point. He wants to discourage easy religion with its false sense of certainty. How easy it is to believe the latest trend or popular fad simply because the crowd promotes it. The source could be from the pulpit or from the media, but the effect is the same: destruction of the soul. Limiting or eliminating self-examination is key to walking the broad road of destruction. For if one asks, "why am I going this direction?" and begins to analyze one's life measured against the commands of Jesus, a signpost will appear ahead. This signpost will say something to the effect of "Destruction – this way," pointing down one's present path and "Life with Jesus – that way," pointing at a 90 degree angle away from Destruction Road.

The crowd will almost always forbid honest self-examination. It spoils the party on the way to Destruction. After all, they do not know Destruction is their destination. Two different groups travel the same road. One group calls the path "Enjoying Life." They do not raise the issue of self-examination because it can detract from the pleasure of the journey down such a broad, well-paved road. The second group discourages self-examination because they have a system all figured out for making it to the destination. It involves following the rules someone has already thought out for you. Self-examination spoils the system because it exposes weaknesses in the proposed solution to every problem. Therefore, it is dangerous to the program and will prevent the group from arriving safely at Destruction, which they believe is Paradise.

Apparently, it is indeed difficult to travel on the path leading to Life. It requires honest self-examination with Jesus as the reference point. It would be much easier if it simply required Jesus as the reference point. Then it would be only a matter of believing the right things *about* Jesus rather than actually *following* Jesus. The self-examiner asks the questions: "Can I see Jesus up ahead? Am I still going in the right direction?" and it involves a willingness to change direction at any time to stay with Jesus.

Questions:

1. What makes Destruction Road such an easy path?

2. What makes Life Road such a difficult and narrow way?

3. Who can help you find the Narrow Gate and the Road to Life?

> *"Beware of false prophets, who come to you in sheep's clothing, but inwardly are ravenous wolves. You will know them by their fruits."*
>
> —Matthew 7:15-16

Jesus warns us to beware of, or watch out for, false prophets. A false prophet is someone purporting to speak the word of God, but instead speaking their own mind or that of someone else. How many ideas are attributed to God which did not really originate with him? How many of our programs and goals really come from him? These are questions worth asking simply because Jesus tells us to beware of false prophets.

He says they come in sheep's clothing. This means they have the appearance of belonging with the flock. They look like they belong with God's people. They are deceptive, and therefore are sons of the chief deceiver, Satan, who is "the father of lies" (John 8:44). What they cannot gain by force, intimidation, or control, they attempt to gain through manipulation of the prophetic voice of God. It is a clever tactic, but one we are not unaware of, thanks to Jesus' warning command.

Inwardly, these people are like hungry wolves. They will surround and tear into shreds the slow, dim-witted, and unaware members of the Church. Picture a pack of wolves surrounding a small calf from a cattle herd or the lionesses pouncing on the slow zebra. They will maneuver and trick an animal until they can devour it and when they take it to the ground, they rip their teeth unmercifully into its flesh. This is what the false prophets will do. They will feed upon you to fill their own ravenous hunger; they are predators who cannot and will not do otherwise.

But since they are so deceptive and have such good camouflage, how can we know who they are? How can we avoid them? Jesus gives us the answer: "You will know them by their fruits." You will see the results of their actions. A member of the flock does not stalk stealthily in the tall grass. God's people do not rip and tear to fill their own bellies, to satisfy their cravings. They do not display a predatory instinct. This is the work of the animal nature, not the character of God. The best way to watch out for them turns out to be simply knowing God's character so well you can instantly spot a counterfeit. You will see the stalking behavior, the traps, the isolation of the prey, and be able to avoid it. A watchful zebra can run with the herd before the lions can isolate it from its companions. Together, they have been known to actually fight off lion attacks. Singly, no zebra is a match for its predator, but no lion will risk injury or death at the hooves of the entire herd.

Do not allow yourself to become isolated from other Christians. Not only is this good theology, it is vital for your own survival. Watch out for the young and the weak. Warn them when you see predators approaching. Teach them how to discern for themselves the movements of the wolves and lions: the twitching of the grass; lying in wait; pouncing on unwary prey. Teach them what a real Christian looks like. Help them become familiar with the voice of our shepherd, Jesus, and to obey His commands. And always stay connected with Him yourself. Sometimes we lose sight of the shepherd as we wander and graze through the world. At such times we can look for the flock and know the shepherd is not far away. Then run back where the flock is until you see Him.

Questions:

1. What motivates false prophets?

2. What risks are there if we do not heed Jesus' command to watch out for them?

3. What makes a false prophet so dangerous? What are their weapons?

4. How can you identify and avoid them?

> *"Follow Me, and let the dead bury their own dead."*
> —Matthew 8:22

Jesus, confronted with a potential disciple, gives a command which at first appears only to apply to this particular situation. Examined more closely, however, it is applicable to any potential disciple of Jesus. The man wants to follow Jesus, quite literally, along the dusty paths of Palestine. He has a small problem, in that his father is still alive and he has a familial duty to bury his father before he can move on with his own life. His father may or may not have required his care, we do not know. What we do know is this man was aware of his social obligation to his father and rightly brings it before Jesus.

The reply he receives, however, is rather shocking in its disregard for social responsibility. Jesus, perceiving the situation, declares the father is spiritually dead and the rest of the family and relations are also; "let the dead bury their own dead." The father is part of the "dead" because he is called "their own." The family is declared "dead," even though they are physically alive enough to bury a literally dead person. It can mean only one thing: Jesus is making a statement similar to his "you must be born again" statement to Nicodemus in the Gospel of John, chapter 3. He declares what appears to be alive physically, is really spiritually dead. For the young man to become a disciple of Jesus will require him to leave behind the spiritually dead family and its dead obligations and follow Jesus in a new life.

Most of us will try to rationalize this command away in some fashion. We do not want to be seen as disregarding our social obligations. But Jesus has no regard for social obligations when they conflict with a person's ability to become a disciple. How many of us have expectations placed upon us by our families and relatives preventing us from obeying God's call to discipleship? Perhaps this expectation is for a certain career path or education. Or maybe we are expected to continue the family business. These goals, in themselves are not evil, but becoming an obstacle to complete obedience to Jesus makes them "dead weight." They weigh us down with concerns about what others think of us rather than what Jesus thinks of us. They force us to consider the priorities of a spiritually dead world before the priorities of the Living God. In this, they are definitely a deceitful, evil temptation.

This man may have walked away from the opportunity to follow Jesus really and personally, to become like the other disciples in their radical obedience to Jesus. All he had to do was put one foot in front of the other and walk after Jesus. Instead, the weight of those spiritually dead obligations may have prevented him from taking the first step and entering into the full life Jesus wants for us all. The irony of the situation is Jesus told him the solution: "let the dead bury their own dead." In other words, the spiritually dead will take care of those dead obligations in our absence. If they do not, they simply show how unimportant those obligations really are to them. And if those obligations are so unimportant, then why should they be used as a way of keeping us from following Jesus as fully committed disciples? The logic is inescapable: either they will perform those dead obligations for us, thus freeing us to follow Jesus, or they will not perform those obligations and show those obligations are not so important after all.

There is, however, another kind of obligation. This is an obligation of love. If someone in my family is ill and requires my assistance because there is no one else to help, will I be there for them even if it means giving up my dreams? Perhaps, in such cases, there is something more than a "dead obligation." How would we treat someone who was not a family member in such cases? Would we serve them in love? If this is the case, then what is faced is an obligation of love. Their claim to our service does not rest solely on familial relationship or social obligation, but rather on the fact they are a human being in need and we are in their closest network of people available to help them. There is no black and white rule allowing us to make decisions in every case. A sensitivity to the Spirit of God is necessary. But the thrust of Jesus' command is clear: just because society places an obligation upon you does not mean it is an obligation God has placed upon you, regardless of appearances.

Questions

1. Are there expectations and obligations you face from your family or society preventing you from fully following Christ?

2. Which of these obligations are "spiritually dead" and which are "obligations of love"? How can you tell the difference?

3. Would you be willing to repeat the command of Jesus to someone facing a dead obligation and challenge them to follow Christ, even though it could mean division with those closest to them? If not, why not?

"Follow Me."

—Matthew 9:9

This simple command was addressed to Levi, the tax collector who became the disciple Matthew, the author of the Gospel from which it is quoted. It is, however, a general command to every person, as seen in the previous example of the man who wanted to wait and bury his father. What is so striking about this particular example is the immediacy of Jesus' command. It was there in the previous example also, but was not followed by immediate obedience in the obliged son. In the example of Levi, we see him get up immediately from his desk at work and leave to follow Jesus. He goes home and puts on a large supper for Jesus, inviting all his "sinner" friends to meet this man who has changed his life with one simple command.

The immediacy of expected obedience is always there in the commands of Jesus. The only reason for its absence is our lack of faith, of trust that when we obey Him, everything will work out. Matthew shows us not only does it work out, but his life becomes full to an extent never possible before. No one would have ever heard of Levi today if not for his immediate trust in Jesus. He would have been another nameless person in the Gospels like the obliged man in the previous example. Instead, he goes on to become Matthew the Apostle, author of one of the most read books of all time.

This is how important immediate obedience is to Jesus. We are the ones who miss out by delaying. We are the ones who pass up opportunities which will never again present themselves to us in our lives. We do not know what will come of our choices; Levi had no idea he would become Matthew. However, he trusted Jesus and this was all that was required.

To obey this command requires we know where Jesus is going. If we are to follow Him, we must see Him. Levi had the opportunity of seeing Him with his natural eyes. Today we have the opportunity to see Him in the Spirit, to experience Him in a way Levi could not until the day of Pentecost. We can know where Jesus is going by knowing Him intimately, by dwelling with Him in our heart of hearts, or, as the Psalmist says, "the secret place of the Most High" (Psalm 91:1). Then we will be able to follow Him. We do, however, have some written clues as to His general direction. One of them is found in this scripture passage just a few verses down. When the Pharisees question why Jesus would eat supper with Levi's unscrupulous "sinner" friends, Jesus replies, "It is not the healthy who need a doctor, but the sick….For I have come not to call the righteous, but sinners." (Matthew 9:12) So Jesus is busy going where these "sinners" can find healing through the Good News of the Kingdom of God. He is bringing this message to them because they need it. In fact, everyone needs this message, but the self-righteous people do not think they need this message. So Jesus does not push them away (he was sitting there with Pharisees also) but he does not seek them out. Instead, he is looking for people like Levi, who know they are sinners and now have a new option available to them. We should go and do likewise.

Questions

1. Why does Jesus expect our immediate obedience?

2. What does this command mean for us today?

3. Why does Jesus look for people who are sinners? Are there places and situations we can follow Him into today like the tax collector's desk?

4. Have you ever found yourself thinking like the Pharisees in this scripture reference? If so, who was involved and how is Jesus reaching out to them now?

"Go and learn what this means: 'I desire mercy and not sacrifice.'"
—Matthew 9:13

Jesus gives us here a direct assault on every form of human religion ever constructed by anyone, anytime, in any place. For the essence of human religion is its sacrifice. It can be as primitive as the sacrificial offering of an animal or human being to the gods or as subtle as the burning of tobacco over a campfire to make a sweet aroma for the nature spirits. The accretion of human tradition on the pure commands of the living God does not escape this criticism either. It tells us we must do such-and-such on certain days in certain ways in order to gain God's favor or to be truly spiritual.

To all this, Jesus says simply we should go investigate what the scriptures had already told us by the prophet Hosea (6:6). In particular, Jesus is addressing the Pharisees, who complain at his eating with sinners at Levi's dinner party. The point is broader, however, in Jesus' mind. The whole Pharisee way of thinking is off track. In order for them to understand why he would choose to eat supper with sinners, they must first understand God's heart. The shocking thing is, it's been there all the time in the Bible: God does not care one bit about any sacrifice or anything you give to Him. What He cares about is when you display His character: mercy. This is what pleases the living God: to see us be like Him. After all, He made us originally "in His own image" (Genesis 1:27).

The command of Jesus here is clear. We need to learn for ourselves what God means when he says he desires "mercy not sacrifice." It is not a rule we can follow or a religious observance. He is commanding us to establish a living relationship with God through His character and with others by showing His character to them. Thus, for Jesus to eat with the sinners shows how God sees them. It is God Himself eating with them. He is commanding us to be like God and have God's attitudes towards others.

Questions

1. Why would God not care about our sacrifices?

2. Why does God desire mercy?

3. Why is it easier for us to sacrifice than it is to be merciful?

"Pray the Lord of the harvest to send out laborers into His harvest."

—Matthew 9:38

In this command, Jesus tells us directly one item for which we are to pray specifically. We are to ask God to send out people willing to reap the harvest he has prepared. In context, Jesus is traveling all through the towns and villages of Israel, teaching and preaching. He sees the great crowds of people coming to hear his preaching and receive his healing. This moves him with compassion and the sense these people are leaderless and looking for someone to lead them into the Kingdom of God. Jesus says they are like "sheep without a shepherd (Matthew 9:36)

His next statement is the harvest is so plentiful, but the laborers so few. He recognizes preaching the Kingdom of God and demonstrating its healing power is larger than even he could accomplish in a single human body. It is even larger than his disciples can handle. In fact, it is so large, he specifically tells us to pray God would send out workers to accomplish this task. This means the situation is so desperate, no willing worker would be turned away. Everyone who *will* answer the call *is* called.

Even if there is something which prevents us from traveling to far countries or preaching to the crowds of people who have never heard the message of the Kingdom of God, Jesus is showing us a point of action every Christian is capable of performing. We can *pray* for God to send those who *can* go to preach and teach. We can ask Him to send us if it is His will and we can let others see the need Jesus saw when he had compassion on the crowds. In this way, we can both obey his command and begin to develop the same heart of compassion he has for those who are "harassed and helpless, like sheep without a shepherd."

Questions:

1. Have you ever wondered if you are called to go and preach, teach, and demonstrate the Kingdom of God?

2. Would you be willing to earnestly ask God to send workers, perhaps even *you,* to the harvest fields?

3. Would you be willing to make *this* job of preaching the Kingdom of God the primary focus of your life and all other jobs secondary to its accomplishment?

4. Is there any less of a need for laborers in God's harvest today?

"As you go, preach, saying, 'the kingdom of heaven has drawn near.'"

—Matthew 10:7

Here, Jesus smashes many of the excuses arising from our feelings of inadequacy about how to preach the Gospel. He simply tells us to say, "the kingdom of heaven has drawn near." It is a very direct and explicit statement. Interestingly, this statement says nothing explicit about Jesus, sin, atonement, or any of the essential elements of the Gospel. It starts from a broader perspective before it addresses human need. The Gospel of the Kingdom is not simply a way of making life bearable, even though it definitely does so. It does not simply address our felt or very real needs. Before all of that, the Gospel of the Kingdom of God is the *truth*.

Aleksandr Solzhenitsen wrote the stunning novel, *The Gulag Archipelago,* about the human experience in Soviet concentration camps. In this novel, he set out the conclusion that even in the most repressive system, the truth will eventually prevail if it is proclaimed. Repressive societies are possible because people are afraid to speak the truth; they are afraid to voice what everyone knows is wrong. This keeps them divided and controllable; they keep their heads down so they do not end up in jail or killed.

Satan has enslaved the human race in a repressive world system based on sin. He keeps everyone in denial about its impact and even its existence. One can go on living in this repressive system until death unless someone tells the truth about it. Jesus' instruction to us is to say the Kingdom of heaven not only exists, but has drawn near to the listeners.

The Resistance has finally come to let you know you live in a country occupied by a foreign invader with no right to rule over you. The rightful King has come and he has dealt with the power of the invader. The Christian who bears the message of the Gospel is a representative of the Resistance movement. By speaking the truth about the reality of our occupation, a beginning is made to find a way of escape and active resistance.

While it is still possible for the listener to ignore the truth, it is impossible to deny someone has told them the truth. They may even choose to live the lie rather than the truth simply because it is psychologically easier. If one is not ready to admit there is a lie, then one will certainly not affirm the truth. All our preaching about sin, the death of Jesus on the cross of Calvary to save us, and the offer of salvation to everyone will be rejected if this basic admission is not made first. One must be ready to follow the truth wherever it leads, regardless of the consequences. Jesus knew this and instructed his disciples to begin by simply announcing the reality of the true Kingdom's arrival.

Questions

1. What difference does it make to first think of the Gospel of the Kingdom of heaven as the truth?

2. Why does oppression depend on lies and how does the proclamation of the truth bring liberty?

3. How does thinking about the Gospel as the truth keep you from worrying about how the message will be received?

4. What difference would it make to your personal evangelism if you saw yourself as a member of a wartime resistance movement fighting against an oppressive invader?

"Heal the sick, cleanse the lepers, raise the dead, cast out demons. Freely you have received, freely give."
—Matthew 10:8

After preaching the message of truth about the Kingdom of God, Jesus tells us to give. The strange thing for us is this giving he is talking about has nothing to do with money, but everything to do with giving to others what God has given to us. Has God set you free from a demon of alcoholism? Help others be free also. Has God healed you of sickness and disease? Be part of someone else's healing. Were you an outcast and made welcome in God's family? Go find others who are also outcasts and bring them in. Perhaps you felt "dead" in your sin, numb to life, and unable to find any hope in the world. There are many people like you. When God sets you free, raises you from death to life, brings you close to himself, he does it as a free gift, but he does not do it without a reason. He does it because he loves you and because he wants to use you, just like those disciples he addressed in this scripture passage, to reach others in the world with these same gifts.

Do we have any right to feel better than others because God has chosen to heal us or forgive us or bring us into relationship with himself? Not at all! Instead, God seems to seek out those people who know they are in trouble, know they can't handle life; they are in way over their heads. In many cases, he intervenes miraculously to change something in a powerful way. Then he gives you power to go and do the same for others, not so you can be recognized for how important you are, but so the work he started in you is carried to completion in others. "Freely you have received, freely give."

There is another way of looking at this from a selfish point of view. One can acknowledge the blessings God has given and think of them as an opportunity for advancement of oneself in the world. God saved you from sin so you can be successful. Perhaps success comes as a side benefit, but it is not the emphasis Jesus gives in this command. His focus is on the gracious, undeserving nature of God's gift to you and the expectation you will now have something to give others. In fact, by pouring out what you have to give, you may not become successful at all, at least in terms the world would consider "success." The standards or measures of success are different. Generally, the world will measure success by the amount of money in your bank account. Even fame is only beneficial if it translates to increased wealth because of your popularity.

By following Jesus' command to give what you have received freely, you may never become rich by the world's standards. God may continue to give you money or fame or blessings, but you continue giving them out as fast as you receive them. They never quite seem to accumulate in your account, but when you step back and look at the wealth which has passed through your fingers to others, you realize what has been happening: you are a venture capitalist for the Kingdom of God, you are financing the growth of the Kingdom in others.

I am using the analogy of money because this is how the world measures wealth, but the blessings you pass on may not be measured in paper currency. Think, however, what it takes to pay someone to care for a sick person. Now, if you are doing this freely, out of love, this person is receiving the benefit of something the world may value in thousands of dollars. Yet, all you did was give several hours a day to bathe them and change their sheets and sit and talk with them. Are you beginning to see the wealth God has given you to share with others? It is Jesus' command to us to share this wealth with others and spread it around freely, the way he did for us.

When you catch hold of this, you will realize you have the equivalent of millions of dollars to share with others. You are the source of more wealth than Bill Gates or Donald Trump or anyone else who has an enormous bank account. What are the chances their wealth will find its way to the elderly person down the block from you? Now, what are the chances they will receive the wealth God has given you to share with those you encounter in life?

Questions:

1. What has God given you freely?

2. Have you ever shared it with someone who needed it?

3. What was the result of your sharing?

4. How can you measure your net worth besides the size of your bank account?

5. Is it optional for us to give what God has given us?

"Behold, I send you out as sheep in the midst of wolves. Therefore, be wise as serpents and harmless as doves."
—Matthew 10:16

"Get behind me, Satan! You are an offense to me, for you are not mindful of the things of God, but the things of men."
—Matthew 16:23

Jesus makes a statement of fact about the way he sends us out into the world to share the Gospel with others. We are like sheep going out among wolves. A loving heart can be in great danger if it is naïve. It goes out thinking people will want to receive its love, welcome the outpouring of God's grace, and be happy to meet a person full of the love of God. Sheep can be clueless about reality. They simply feed all day and are unaware of the predators lurking at the edge of the forest, waiting to feast on them.

A young heart full of the love of God can be like these sheep. Jesus is commanding us not to be naïve. He tells us to "be wise as serpents and harmless as doves." Be aware the world treated Jesus badly, refused his message, and even his miracles, and they will do the same to you. Watch out, then, so you will not be devoured. Do not allow the opposition and the battles to harden your heart and make you cynical. Cynicism begins as naiveté and eventually crowds out your faith. It can be fatal.

It is possible, however, to be aware of the sin in the world and still go out to love it. In fact, this is what Jesus did. He knew full well he was going to be crucified at the right time and he allowed it to happen to fulfill the purposes of God. He was not an unwilling victim. In other words, he could have stopped it at any time if he wanted. He actually did escape several times when crowds wanted to kill him; it was not the proper time yet.

When you go out into the world bearing the Gospel, be aware of the purposes God is fulfilling in you. Do not think you are the answer to every problem. Know what God is doing through you. People will try to take advantage of your love, they will abuse your offer of relationship, and attempt to manipulate you to achieve their own ends. In some cases, you may feel it is God's purpose to allow these things to happen to accomplish a greater Kingdom goal in their lives. Most of the time, however, it is simply a display of their selfish, sinful nature. Do not be fooled into compromising your mission to them by their attempts to use you for their own purposes.

"Now while he was in Jerusalem at the Passover Feast, many people saw the miraculous signs he was doing and believed in his name. But Jesus would not entrust himself to them, for he knew all men. He did not need man's testimony about man, for he knew what was in a man." (John 2:23-25)

Here Jesus shows us even though people were ready to give him great fame, which had the potential to increase the size and scope of his ministry, he did not try to leverage this. He knew it could easily be used against him. He was committed to accomplishing God's purposes God's way. Do not be fooled by the wolves as you engage the world with the Gospel. Sometimes they have an appearance of friendship or they only want to help. Jesus was equally harsh with one of his best friends when he wanted to "help" Jesus make what he thought were better decisions.

"From that time on Jesus began to explain to his disciples that he must go to Jerusalem and suffer many things at the hands of the elders, chief priests and teachers of the law, and that he must be killed and on the third day be raised to life.

Peter took him aside and began to rebuke him. 'Never, Lord!' he said. 'This shall never happen to you!' Jesus turned and said to Peter, 'Get behind me, Satan! You are a stumbling block to me; you do not have in mind the things of God, but the things of men.'" (Matthew 16:21-23)

Here we have a command Jesus addressed to Satan, through Peter. He realized it was not Peter who came up with this advice to disregard the purposes of God in his life. So Jesus confronted Satan by commanding him to get out of his way. Peter was probably hurt and shocked by this (I would be!), but Jesus said it anyway. He probably wanted Peter to see how Satan was using his sinful desire to come up with a human solution to the perceived problem of Jesus not choosing what Peter thought was the best course of action. In effect, this harsh command to Satan, addressed to Peter, was a loving act toward Peter. It made him more aware of Satan's scheme to use him to divert Jesus from God's will.

In any case, what is important is knowing the will of God and doing it. Do not be swayed by clever arguments or manipulation of personal relationships. It is a reality we must confront about people in general and requires a level of wisdom Jesus compares to a serpent. Still, he wants us to remain "harmless as doves." This means our wisdom is never used to hurt people. While we may be aware of their scheming and manipulation, we continue to work for their good. We overlook it to the extent we are not offended by it. We do not allow it to sidetrack our ministry work for them because it would then prevent us from serving them as God wants.

Entering into ministry this way has many benefits. It allows you to remain focused on what God has called you to do rather than what others will expect from you. It keeps you from losing faith in God when you see the deceitfulness of men and the extent of evil in the world. It keeps our hearts tender towards

God because we know he experienced all this and more, including complete betrayal, simply to accomplish our salvation from sin. Seeing one soul freed from sin makes it all worth the effort!

Questions:

1. Why does Jesus compare his disciples to sheep among wolves?

2. How can obedience to this command keep us from losing faith in God?

3. How can obedience to this command keep our service to others from getting off-track?

4. Who can be used to manipulate us?

5. What part of this attempted manipulation should we overlook?

"Beware of men, for they will deliver you up to councils and scourge you in their synagogues....when they deliver you up, do not worry about how or what you should speak."
—Matthew 10:17, 19

"When they bring you to synagogues and magistrates and authorities, do not worry about how or what you should answer, or what you should say."
—Luke 12:11

"Therefore, settle it in your hearts not to meditate beforehand on what you will answer; for I will give you a mouth and wisdom which all your adversaries will not be able to contradict or resist."
—Luke 21:14

After the command to "be wise as serpents" regarding the sinfulness of men, Jesus tells us to beware of men. Be suspicious of them, question their motives in your heart, because they will betray you. Do not entrust your soul to them; instead, trust God.

He tells us they will whip us, beat us, publicly humiliate us before councils, seats of authority, courts, and even in centers of religious worship. Now, if you are trusting the government of your country is going to protect your preaching of the Gospel, think again. The supposed "religious tolerance" of the United States is being used to silence people of faith from ever speaking out in public. They will not call it that, however, but the goal is for you to censor yourself. They don't want you to get too radical, nor to speak out what you perceive to be the truth God has spoken, if it could possibly offend someone.

If you think your religious denomination will protect your living out the Gospel, think again. From the religious leaders of Jesus' synagogue to the leaders of many mainline Christian denominations today, religious leaders have been at the forefront of suppressing the public living of the Gospel. It may not seem like outright persecution, but the more subtle forms of manipulation often seem to work best, such as watering down the truth to make it more acceptable or refraining from criticizing aspects of culture which contradict the teaching of the Gospel. When subtle manipulation fails, however, you will see the brutal hand of legal maneuvering and arguments over church properties. Preachers of the Gospel may be removed from the pulpit or marginalized so they have little public audience for their message. Jesus warns they will even scourge you "in their synagogues", right in church!

Jesus then gives his answer to this reality. Instead of entrusting ourselves to men, their authority, their power, their influence, trust in God. Do not worry what you will say, how you will answer their accusations, or about defending your reputation. This trust in God makes one invincible. If we truly trust God, not even the full authority of the government's ability to kill us or place us in jail can threaten us. Jesus showed this when he confronted Pilate.

"Meanwhile, Jesus stood before the governor, and the governor asked him, 'Are you the king of the Jews?'

'Yes, it is as you say,' Jesus replied.

When he was accused by the chief priests and the elders, he gave no answer. Then Pilate asked him, 'Don't you hear the testimony they are bringing against you?' But Jesus made no reply, not even to a single charge – to the great amazement of the governor." (Matthew 27:11-13)

Questions:

1. Why does Jesus tell us to "Beware of men"?

2. Can we trust in institutions to protect us?

3. Will we trust God when we encounter persecution because of the Gospel?

4. What example did Jesus set for us in this?

"When they persecute you in this city, flee to another."
—Matthew 10:23

Note this command begins with an assumption. It does not say, "*If* they persecute you in this city...." Instead, Jesus says, "*When* they persecute you...." He assumes the fact of persecution. If you are faithfully living out the Gospel and telling others about Jesus and his message of the Kingdom of God, be assured, you *will* be persecuted. The persecution may come from people you never expected: the church, the government, local business people, or even your family. So we should not pass over the assumption of Jesus in this command because it is uncomfortable. If we do, we will tend to think persecution happens to "other people" and we will be tempted to compromise the Gospel in order to avoid the persecution when it begins to target us. Do not avoid persecution. Because of Jesus' statement, we know we will not need to look for persecution, it will find us if we are faithful to the message of the Kingdom of God he has given us to bear for him in the world.

Assuming this persecution then, what are we to do when it occurs? There are several responses Christians have tried in history other than the one Jesus commands in this order. One response is to fight back. Use all of your clout, intelligence, political power, rhetorical skill, or any other resource at your disposal to counterattack the persecution. This is particularly tempting for Americans, as we are trained to stick up for our rights from a very young age. It is part of our culture. This is usually a big mistake. While we may win tactical battles in the courts or arguments on television news shows, we miss the point of the response Jesus has given us. He commanded us to flee to another city when we face this persecution. He is, perhaps, concerned about our survival and a popular proverb does teach us "discretion is the greater part of valor." In other words, running from a fight can be a very good survival strategy. The animal kingdom employs this method quite frequently. Most animals, even the most fearsome predators, will usually run if threatened. We could learn quite a bit from animals when it comes to survival.

Jesus, however, is concerned with more than our mere survival, however. He wants the message of the Kingdom of God preached to the whole world. If we refuse to move to another city when persecuted, we may be interfering with God's plan to use us to reach a household, a neighborhood, a city, or a region with the Gospel. The early Church spread the Gospel throughout the ancient world because of their persecution in Jerusalem by the ruling elders. After the day of Pentecost, they used to gather daily at the Temple in its outer courtyard to hear the teaching of the apostles (Acts 2:46). As a result of the stoning of the martyr Stephen, all believers except the apostles ran to surrounding cities and lived out the Gospel there. "On that day a great persecution broke out against the church at Jerusalem, and all except the apostles were scattered throughout Judea and Samaria." (Acts 8:1) Certainly, this was for their survival, but it also had the effect of producing churches in surrounding cities. Those cities may not have had a community of Kingdom-minded people living there had it not been for the persecution in Jerusalem.

Another response Christians have tried to persecution is "going underground." When the heat of persecution gets too much to bear, this strategy is to simply be quiet, not upset the authorities or your family or whoever is persecuting you. It can be an effective survival strategy. Some animals do this by burrowing in the ground. Unfortunately, this seldom works. The reason it fails is in order for a disciple of Jesus to be the person God is making them in Christ, they cannot be stealthy like a submarine. It is impossible to be a "secret believer" for very long. The world will demand you conform to its ways and you will either begin to compromise your integrity as a believer or you will be discovered. Kingdom Christianity cannot be hidden very long.

The danger of this strategy for the believer is it imperils your own faith. It is possible for you to choose compromise so often you become indistinguishable from the culture around you. This is very dangerous for you. In order to blend in and camouflage yourself, you become like those around you. Instead of being faithful to Jesus and making disciples of them, they are making you more and more like the world system. It would have been better to flee as Jesus commanded! At least then you would not have to become a chameleon.

A third alternative to Jesus' command is to simply conform to what the persecuting people demand. They want you to turn in the Jews to the Nazi party authorities, so you do it. They tell you to stop worshiping God openly or using the name of Jesus in your prayers, so you do. They ask you to join the church run by the Communist Party and worship there, so you do. Perhaps they only want you to give up a silly scientific theory that the Earth revolves around the Sun, so you recant. This alternative never has seemed very attractive. In fact, it seems more cowardly than running away. At least, if you simply run, you maintain the integrity of your faith. A little damage to your personal pride from running away seems much better than groveling just so you can remain at home.

In all, the order Jesus gives makes complete sense. But even if we disagree, who are we to argue with our Lord? How could we possibly think we know better?

Another set of commands from Jesus regarding the destruction of Jerusalem also apply in general to this issue of running away from persecution and violence.

"*Therefore, when you see the 'abomination of desolation,' spoken of by Daniel the prophet, standing in the holy place, then let those who are in Judea flee to the mountains. Let him who is on the housetop not go down to take anything out of his house, and let him who is in the field not go back to get his clothes.*"
—Matthew 24:20

"*By your patience possess your souls. But when you see Jerusalem surrounded by armies, then know that its desolation is near. Then let those who are in the midst of her depart, and let not those who are in the country enter her.*"
—Luke 21:19-21

"*Pray that your flight may not be in winter or on the Sabbath.*"
—Matthew 24:20

While Jesus gave specific instructions to his disciples what to do when certain events occurred in the future, we cannot be sure they apply to every disciple because not every disciple will be in Jerusalem to observe these events. We all gain insight, however, by examining his command how to respond to these events. It is interesting he did not tell his disciples to stand and fight for Jerusalem, which would have a certain heroic appeal. Jesus will be coming back triumphantly at the end of history and what better way to greet him than with sword in hand, fighting for the holy city? Suddenly he will appear at the last moment when all seems hopeless and lead us to conquer our enemies. It reads like the script of a final battle scene in an epic film.

Instead, Jesus tells his disciples to run away! He even tells them not to go into the house for a change of clothes, but rather run for your lives. He prophesies there is no way to avoid this flight, it is going to happen. The best we can do is be patient and keep our wits about us. "By your patience, you will possess your souls." Someone in possession of his soul is in control and aware what is happening in the moment of crisis. He knows exactly what to do and is not shocked or dismayed to the extent it keeps him from taking action.

The only thing we can do about this horrible event Jesus foretold is to pray. He told us to pray the flight would not be in winter or on the Sabbath. This would be difficult because in winter, it gets cold and if you obeyed him and did not go back for a change of clothes, you probably would not be well protected from the environment. The Sabbath would also be a difficult time to run, since everything would be geared toward resting. You would be even less prepared to flee in this state of mind. So the best we can do at times is to pray our difficulties, like this predicted flight, will not be as bad as they could be. And we can remember Jesus' command is for us to run!

Questions:

1. What does Jesus mean by "persecution?"

2. Why does Jesus assume his disciples will be persecuted?

3. How does each of the three alternative options compromise the integrity of a disciple?

4. Looking back at your life, have you ever chosen one of the other options when faced with persecution? How did it turn out?

5. Does fleeing to another city necessarily mean geographical relocation? How will your answer affect your faithfulness to Jesus?

6. What specific instructions did Jesus give to his disciples as to how they are to react to the impending destruction of Jerusalem? How can these apply to every disciple, even those not present during this specific historical event?

"If they have called the master of the house Beelzebub, how much more will they call those of his household! Therefore, do not fear them."

—Matthew 10:25-26

"Whatever I tell you in the dark, speak in the light; and what you hear in the ear, preach on the housetops. And do not fear those who kill the body but cannot kill the soul. But rather fear him who is able to destroy both soul and body in hell."

—Matthew 10:27-28

Jesus warns us people will call us, his disciples, the worst names imaginable. In fact, they called him Beelzebub, which was the pagan lord of the flies, a first-rank evil devil. People will say you are of the devil if you begin to live and preach what Jesus taught; make no mistake about it. Why?

Perhaps because so much of what Jesus taught undermines what we think we know about God. It certainly prevents us from making God who we want him to be. This is a sure sign of the true and Living God who revealed himself through history in the bible: he is not what we want him to be, he is who he is. The only way we can know God is by him revealing himself to us. This is the God Moses met through the burning bush (Exodus 3:1-14). It is the God Jesus claims as his father. Jesus goes even farther and tells us no one can even know God the Father except those to whom the Son reveals him (Matthew 11:27).

This is a very intimidating claim. It means all religion is useless in knowing God except as taught by Jesus. No wonder the religious authorities wanted to kill Jesus! And no wonder they will call you the devil himself if you preach and live as Jesus did.

Jesus' response to this is to command us to "preach on the housetops." He wants us to openly declare everything he has commanded. He commands us "do not fear them," the ones who slander you and want to injure you. In fact, he even contrasts their pitiful power to kill you with the power God has to both kill and throw into hell. The implied question is, "who do you think you should be afraid of, those people slandering and threatening you, or God?" He does not frame it as a question though. Instead, it is a command: "Do not fear [them], rather fear [God]."

Some very interesting things begin to happen in your life when you obey this command. Suddenly, the authority you thought was so important to your future, the people around you, their opinions of you and their thoughts of what your life should look like, become less important. You become more *free* to be who God is making you. This brings greater opposition from them because people like to exercise control over other people. The most extreme form of control is one a government uses: the threat of force or imprisonment. There are, however, more subtle and effective methods such as controlling the information you have to make decisions, telling you how you should think about a certain topic, and influencing your behavior through approval and disapproval. When you begin to care more about what God thinks than what people think of you, the softer forms of power people exercise over your life begin to become ineffective. They will then turn to the harder, more physical methods of power: bullying, name-calling, isolation, imprisonment, and even death. If you think I am being a little too extreme, look at the life of Jesus and how the authorities responded to him and his disciples. They first tried to get them to stop preaching publicly. Then, when they realized this would not work, they said Jesus and his teaching were demonic. Later, when that failed to stop the spread of this Jesus-teaching, they beat him and killed him. The same happened to his disciples.

This should not be surprising because Jesus himself tells us it is so in these scriptures from Matthew 10. His command to us to fear God instead of people is very important for us. We will inevitably be tempted to compromise the message of our preaching and lives when confronted with the disapproval of powerful people and institutions. Jesus commands us not to compromise. He wants us to be public witnesses of what he has shown us. The amount of faith we have in God determines the level of regard or "fear" we have for him rather than the level of regard for what people say, threaten, or do. It is not only true, but a useful survival skill for disciples who wish to remain free in the liberty Christ gives rather than be held captive by the opinions and power of people.

Questions:

1. Why will people even say you are demonic if you begin to preach and live a life centered on the Gospel?

2. What is Jesus' response to this fact?

3. Think of a time when someone else's opinion influenced you to do something you knew to be against what God wants. Is fear of people a very real, powerful force?

4. How can fear or regard for God counteract the power people will attempt to exert over you?

5. Why is the Gospel of Jesus Christ threatening to every form of power?

> "Do not fear therefore; you are of much more value than many sparrows."
>
> —Matthew 10:31

We saw in the previous Standing Order Jesus wants us to fear God. This is not a religious, manipulative fear. Instead, he wants us to regard what God wants more highly than what people want, even people who may be religious or political authorities. These authorities sometimes use our fear of their power and reputation to manipulate us for their own purposes. God is not manipulative. He clearly states what he wants from us and even sent his only son, Jesus, to show us what he meant.

This next Standing Order shows God does not want us to be *afraid* of anything, even for our future. He tells us we are worth much more than the little birds God knows individually. God cares about us individually. When we begin to realize this and actually *believe* it, something important changes in how we handle life. We used to worry about how we will live, what our income will be, who will care for us in old age. These concerns are common to all people, in every age.

Jesus, however, commands us to live differently, with a conviction God actually cares about us enough to ensure we will have everything we need and more. The previous Standing Order made us free from the manipulation of people based on our fear of them. Obedience to this Standing Order liberates us from our own concerns and worries about life and its basic necessities. He encourages us to look to our loving Father for these things rather than make our own plans. Jesus is saying, in effect, "you are not on your own in life."

While Jesus assures us God is for us and with us, he does not tell us *how* our Father plans to provide for our needs. What is more important for us is to be obedient to God, to show regard for what he wants, to spend our energy on his pursuits rather than insuring our ability to pursue our desires. This is an incredibly liberating order! We are free from the manipulation of others, but we are also now free from the manipulation of ourselves. Instead we can be fully ready to serve God in any way he chooses.

Some people actually enjoy worrying about their future and providing for their needs. It gives them a sense of purpose and a false sense of security. They think if they can only be totally independent, then life will be good. The sense of this within all of us is seen in movements to "get off the grid", live out in the wilderness in total independence, and be completely self-sufficient. These desires, in themselves are not evil. The myth of total independence is, however. Assume for a moment you had a magic device or advanced technology which provided you with unlimited energy. You could, theoretically, use this energy to produce whatever you want; the only restriction would be in your access to raw materials. Given enough energy and advanced technology, you could, theoretically, produce whatever materials you wanted using nuclear transmutation. Now, living in your island paradise with unlimited energy, food, and materials, why would you need relationship with God? Instead, you would begin to feel like a god. Think of it; unlimited power! No one telling you what you can and cannot do!

This is exactly why we need God and must learn to depend upon him through everyday, normal processes of life. Even if we possessed the power to live independently, we were not created to be independent. God created us to be in relationship with him. Part of that relationship involves us trusting him with our needs in life. Besides, the myth of total independence is a lie. Remember the story *20,000 Leagues Under the Sea*? In it,

Jules Verne imagined a man, Captain Nemo, who discovered an unlimited power source. With this power source, he built a self-contained world aboard a submarine. This submarine was so powerful and independent from the Victorian-age world of the novel's setting, it could sink the warships of the dominant navies and escape. If anyone was ever truly independent, it was Captain Nemo. Jules Verne wrote a sequel, which is much less famous, titled *The Mysterious Island*. At the end of the novel, Captain Nemo admits, as he is dying, he was wrong to think a man can live completely independent from human society. He realized his independence was a lie.

No matter what size your Individual Retirement Account or 401(k) plan is, you will need God's help in providing for your needs. It is better for us if we realize this early in life and get on with the business of living for him first, rather than worrying about padding our accounts for unlimited playtime later. In fact, many people are in effect slaves to their retirement and will work at horrible jobs for decades just to escape into retirement later on. This is a lie! You never know when your life is over, how long you will live, or if you will ever even get to enjoy the retirement account! Jesus told a story of a man who was prosperous and decided to save more for retirement in Luke 12:16-21:

"The ground of a certain rich man yielded plentifully. And he thought within himself, saying, 'What shall I do, since I have no room to store my crops?' So he said, 'I will do this: I will pull down my barns and build greater, and there I will store all my crops and my goods. And I will say to my soul, 'Soul, you have many goods laid up for many years; take your ease, eat, drink, and be merry.'

But God said to him, 'Fool! This night your soul will be required of you; then whose will those things be which you have provided?'

So is he who lays up treasure for himself and is not rich toward God."

If we are "rich toward God", Jesus promised us our Father will see to our every need. We can trust him to do exactly what he says if we give up believing the myth of total independence.

Questions:

1. Have you ever felt manipulated by your own desires and by providing a way to satisfy them rather than following what God wants?

2. How do we know we are not "on our own in life"?

3. What is the "myth of total independence" and how can it be seductive?

4. What can the example of Captain Nemo teach us about it?

5. How does Jesus' story of the rich man and his barns relate to this Standing Order?

> "Whoever confesses me before men, him will I also confess before my Father who is in heaven."
> —Matthew 10:32

This is not technically a command, but it does reveal the will of Jesus. He does not specifically say we are to publicly preach about him, but he does say he will reward those who do. A reward is typically given to reward behavior you want to encourage. For example, you offer a child a treat when they complete their schoolwork in a satisfactory manner. So Jesus is telling us he wants us to tell other people we know him and teach what he taught us. He says for those who do this, he will also tell his Father in heaven he knows you and approves of you.

The converse is also true: "whoever denies me before men, him I will also deny before my Father who is in heaven." (Matthew 10:33) You cannot have it both ways. You must choose which approval you want: God's or the world's. Sometimes the world will give its approval to you in a limited sense, until your true colors show as a follower of Jesus. This annoying commitment to a dead heretical rabbi and his teaching will inevitably conflict with the priorities of the human world. It is best to make up your mind **now** where your commitment lies.

Jesus is up front about his desire for your commitment to him and he does not hide the consequences of denial either. He places the choice squarely in our laps with full knowledge of the consequences. All maneuvering around this statement ignores the clear intentions of Jesus. The only option if Jesus embarrasses you is to ignore this statement. We do so, however, at the risk of Jesus being embarrassed of us before God!

Return to the analogy of a watch officer using the Captain's Standing Orders. There is one reason for those Orders: to indicate the Captain's will to the officer in likely situations. They are commands in the strict sense, but they are also implicit windows into the mind of the Captain. You learn what he thinks is important by reading his Standing Orders. Different captains have different priorities and no two sets of Standing Orders are the same. For the disciple of Jesus, however, there is only one set of Standing Orders that matters, only one set of intentions that counts – those of Jesus. A disciple who wishes to please his Lord will look farther than simply obeying every direct command Jesus gave. He or she will become so familiar with the Standing Orders they will begin to think like Jesus. This allows them to apply the priorities of Jesus to situations he never addressed.

We do not know what form the temptation to be embarrassed of Jesus will take in our lives. It is probably different for everyone. Certainly one common experience will be with our family members who are not followers of Jesus. We will be tempted to gain their approval because we love them, but their disapproval of Jesus and his teaching will force us to choose whether we will "confess" Jesus publicly or simply hide him under our shirt for our private moments of prayer and meditation.

Questions:

1. What does Jesus mean when he talks about "confessing me" before men?

2. Why will any disciple of Jesus be forced to choose between his approval and the world's?

3. Even if this is not technically a direct order, why is it important and how are such implicit instructions valuable to a disciple?

> *"Do not think that I came to bring peace on earth. I did not come to bring peace, but a sword."*
> —Matthew 10:34

We saw in the last Standing Order we will be forced to choose between the approval of God and human approval. Jesus now makes it very plain and direct. He tells us not to think he "came to bring peace on earth." He says he came for the exact opposite reason, to bring a sword. The sword symbolizes war and division. It is not a peaceful tool and has no use except warfare. It cannot even be used for hunting. The warfare Jesus is talking about is not earthly warfare, however. It is the setting of "a man against his father, a daughter against her mother." (Matthew 10:35) This means, in other words, the opposition of family and friends. They will oppose you because of your public acknowledgement of Jesus and his teaching. You will be an embarrassment to them because the human world does not approve of Jesus' teaching; at least not in its entirety. The world would rather pick and choose those elements it likes and either discard or ignore the rest, especially those appearing harsh or demand changing our ways.

Many people would like to confine Jesus into a manageable deity. "Peace on earth, good will toward men!" (Luke 2:14) is the sum total of this partial gospel. Truly, the army of angels that appeared for the shepherds did say this to them about the birth of Jesus. What is left out often is how this peace and good will were accomplished. The Passion, Death, and Resurrection of Christ were painful, divisive experiences. The peace came at a very expensive price and the good will God has toward all people was displayed in the form of an embarrassing public execution. The Gospel, which is truly "good news", defines everything around these central facts. It is how Jesus himself defined them. Why else would he point out the pain and division his ministry would bring?

If Jesus did not come to bring "peace on earth", then neither do we. Our goal is not to change the world system to make it "Christian." Every attempt to do this in history has failed. The simple fact is people are sinful. The system will corrupt you before you change it. Instead, the mission of Jesus was to offer a different way, an alternative system, a new Kingdom. This Kingdom views the power of the world system indifferently, at best. Where it conflicts with the world system, it acknowledges sharp division, open warfare, a "sword".

The world focuses on changing systems, groups, and institutions, since this is where its power lies. The Kingdom focus is individuals—their liberty from sin and restoration to relationship with God. Because of this, the division strikes very close to home, often cutting across family lines. Face it—we rarely have the opportunity to disagree with political leaders and engage them in conversation about topics that matter. We have daily contact with individual human beings: fathers, mothers, sisters, and brothers. Jesus knows this and makes it very plain for his disciples. Do not be shocked by the conflict, it comes naturally when you are busy expanding the Kingdom of God the way Jesus commanded it be done.

Questions:

1. Why is it popular to think Jesus came to bring peace on earth?

2. How is Jesus' command very realistic rather than idealistic?

3. Jesus, in effect, is telling us what to think. Do you dislike this? Or do you welcome it? Why?

4. Why do attempts to make the world system "Christian" always fail? What is the weak link in the chain?

5. What is the Kingdom view of the world system?

"When Jesus finished commanding His twelve disciples...."
—Matthew 11:1

"He who has ears to hear, let him hear!"
—Matthew 11:15

After issuing a long series of Standing Orders in the first few chapters of the Gospel of Matthew, Jesus concludes with one last command. He says whoever "has ears to hear" should listen to the commands he just gave. Another way of saying the same thing would be: "if you want to listen to what I have to tell you, then listen and put into practice the things you hear." There is nothing more annoying than having a child ask for your advice about something and then go do what they wanted to in the first place! It is as if they want some validation for their course of action by asking your opinion. If your opinion conflicts with their desires, it still can make them feel better they asked and they can go on their merry way doing what they had intended all along.

Jesus tells us not to be this way. He says if we want to hear what he commands, then we should also take those commands to heart and live in this manner. It is not enough to simply physically hear the sounds coming from his mouth, or the preaching from the pulpit, or read the words in the Bible.

The "word of God is living and active. Sharper than any double-edged sword, it penetrates even to the dividing soul and spirit, joints and marrow; it judges the thoughts and attitudes of the heart." (Hebrews 4:12) Jesus commands us to take him and his word seriously. It is not like watching television or listening to music; you should not simply listen to it for enjoyment. While it may bring you joy, it is not primarily for your entertainment. You are not the center of this world, God is. His word is the fixed standard, the immovable rock, the objective reference point for all of reality. If you are going to listen to his word, you had better listen the way Jesus commands.

Nothing could be more dangerous spiritually than listening to the word of God in a way which does not involve adapting your life to it. Remember, this is what Jesus thrashed the Pharisees for: "Woe to you, teachers of the law and Pharisees, you hypocrites! You clean the outside of the cup and dish, but inside they are full of greed and self-indulgence." (Matthew 23:25) You can *look* very religious, quote every scripture, and have theological reasoning to support almost anything you want. Inside, however, all your exposure to the word of God has not brought about any change. This happens because the attitude of the listener is not one of *hearing* in the sense Jesus means. They physically heard the words of Jesus, but they did not take them to heart and change their ways. However, the tax collectors and sinners heard in the sense Jesus meant. People like Zacchaeus who, when confronted with Jesus, decided to restore four times what he had stolen from the people he cheated. The word penetrated deep into his heart and showed him what *he* needed to change.

If we approach Jesus any other way, we are fooling ourselves, but we do not fool him. He knows very well what is in us, our capacity for self-deception and hypocrisy. That is why he gives us this direct command to "hear!"

Questions:

1. Why would Jesus command us to "hear" if we have "ears to hear"? If we are listening to him already, is it not enough?

2. Why did Jesus verbally thrash the Pharisees?

3. Is it difficult or easy to do the same thing the Pharisees did?

4. How does the response of a sinner like Zacchaeus show us how the Kingdom of God works in our lives?

5. Why does exposure to the word of God require repentance on our part?

6. Why would television and the entertainment industry in general make this harder for us?

"Come to me, all you who labor and are heavy laden, and I will give you rest. Take my yoke upon you and learn from me, for I am gentle and lowly in heart, and you will find rest for your souls."

—Matthew 11:28-29

For those who are afraid listening to Jesus will be too difficult for them or will require a superhuman effort beyond their ability to respond, Jesus gives this command. He simply orders us to "come to" him. He does not give us a list of do's and don'ts. We see how easily even a good list like the Law of Moses can be twisted to accommodate wicked attitudes and behavior in the example of the Pharisees. The answer of Jesus is very simple, many would say it is *too* simple! If we come to him, personally, one-on-one, as a human being to their Creator, he will give us rest.

This Standing Order comes with a promise. God is putting himself on record to do something for us. He will give us rest. This is the most precious gift he could give. We do not need a new car; we need a way to get around. We do not need a better house; we need the use of shelter. We do not need to make more money; we need to be able to do the things more money will enable us to do. So much of our time and concern is worrying about how we will get and keep the things we want and need in life. Religious people are very concerned with how they will get to heaven. Scholars are concerned about gaining knowledge. What we really need, however is rest, contentment, peace in our hearts.

Jesus has told us elsewhere if we first seek God's kingdom and his righteousness, he will give us everything we need. It requires, however, we come to him. He cannot give us rest from far away. The contentment in life is with him. It extends even beyond the grave into eternity, because he is eternal. In this sense, heaven is not so much a *place* as a state of *being with Jesus*. So we can experience the rest of heaven even here on this terribly wicked world.

There is another element of this Standing Order which brings about our rest. Jesus says we are to take his yoke upon us and learn from him. Most of our lives are spent learning how to survive, how to get what we want. We use this knowledge to work towards our goals. There is great frustration and even depression, however, when things do not quite go as expected. We become burdened by our troubles and our problems become bigger than our solutions. Carried to its logical conclusion, it ends in despair. This is exactly where the world is philosophically right now. Life has no apparent meaning other than what you give to it, so do your best to create some meaning for yourself quickly before you die! There is no one there to comfort you other than fragile, imperfect human beings like yourself. Many times, they do not comfort you but only take advantage of you.

How much better it is to obey Jesus' command to come to him! He will teach us what we need to know in his service. He tells us what kind of master he is: "gentle and lowly in heart." With him, he promises rest for our souls. It may involve unlearning survival lessons from the world system. It definitely will involve implementing the new priorities he will show us. But all this re-arranging of our lives is for our own good! It will result in "rest for your souls."

The basic ingredient of our obedience to Jesus is our trust in him. Do we actually believe he knows what he is doing? In fact, this trusting attitude toward Jesus is the only way we will receive him. There really is no middle ground: you either receive the yoke of Jesus or you remain under a different yoke of your choosing. This is why salvation is so critical for us. Many people are so-called "good people." You may even be one of them. Ultimately, however, we need someone to save us from ourselves. Otherwise, we continue to construct the prison walls of our own despair. Salvation is not simply a one-time event, "asking Jesus into your heart." It begins this way, but it involves a learning process by which we begin to replace our old way of thinking with Jesus' way.

Before they were ever called "Christians" disciples of Christ were known as "followers of the Way." (Acts 9:2; 19:9,23; 22:4; 24:14,22)

Questions:

1. Do you need to broaden your concept of what "salvation" means?

2. What is the only thing Jesus requires we do in this Standing Order?

3. What is the result of our obedience?

4. What is the world's alternative to the rest Jesus offers?

5. Why is it important to know salvation is more than "asking Jesus into your heart"?

6. What difference would it make for you to be called a "follower of the Way" rather than "Christian"?

"It is lawful to do good on the Sabbath."
—Matthew 12:12

This is another one of those implicit Standing Orders. It is not exactly a direct command, but rather a statement of Jesus' intentions regarding proper conduct. The Pharisees have just pointed out to Jesus how his disciples are violating the Sabbath restriction against work by picking grain in the field to eat. Then, Jesus goes into their synagogue and asks them if it is lawful to heal on the Sabbath. There was a man in the synagogue with a shriveled hand.

The Pharisees refused to answer Jesus' question. They knew what the correct answer was and it contradicted their legalistic way of applying the scriptures. So they remained silent. Mark's Gospel says, "He looked around at them in anger and, deeply distressed at their stubborn hearts, said to the man, 'Stretch out your hand.' He stretched it out and his hand was completely restored. Then the Pharisees went out and began to plot with the Herodians how they might kill Jesus." (Mark 3:5-6).

The Pharisee refusal to admit they were wrong in their interpretation of Sabbath laws really put Jesus over the edge of anger and distress. Here he was showing them a man in great need of healing and they refused to allow his life could be changed for good simply because it occurred on the last day of the week! Here, we learn the priorities of Jesus. If we must choose between observing a religious ceremony or holiday and helping people in great need, Jesus says pick helping people. His priority is always people, not unthinking obedience to the rules.

This Standing Order tells us more than we might think at first. It tells us not only about the Sabbath, but how our entire life of worship should be structured. It should be centered on God and his priorities. Even the laws God gives are subordinate to the priorities God has. In effect, Jesus is saying proper interpretation of God's law will always align with God's priority: people. Jesus offered the Pharisees the chance to rightly interpret the law first. He wanted them to admit their rigid interpretation left no room for real people, the people God wants included in his Kingdom.

Jesus was both angry and distressed because they refused to change their faulty application of the law even when presented with a living example of how they were wrong. He literally had the man stand in the center of the synagogue so everyone could see him! By remaining silent, they were denying the basic humanity of a fellow child of God. He was less important to them than admitting they were wrong about a ceremonial point of law. Jesus was distressed not just for the man with the shriveled hand, but also for the Pharisees who were so hard-hearted.

This example shows us the great value God places on individual human beings; they are worth more to him than even his own law! Our priorities should also be the same. People should always come before rigid application of rules. Healing broken people is what Jesus was all about and he is still doing it now through us, his disciples. We should be excited about opportunities to "do good" on the Sabbath because this is what Jesus did.

Questions:

1. Why do you think Sabbath observance was so important to the Pharisees? Are there other rules besides observing the Sabbath that can sometimes conflict with the priority to bring wholeness to broken people?

2. What angered and distressed Jesus so much?

3. Does this give us an indication of the priorities of Jesus? What do you think his priorities are from the scriptures?

4. What if your interpretation of scripture were shown to be wrong? How would you react? What would you use as a basis for determining a correct interpretation?

> *"Therefore hear the parable of the sower:"*
> —Matthew 13:18-23

This command is simple. We are directed to listen to the message of a story Jesus told in the previous verses of the same chapter of Matthew's Gospel. He told his disciples "many prophets and righteous men desired to see what you see and did not see it, and to hear what you hear and did not hear it." *Therefore* they were told to hear Jesus' interpretation of the parable for them.

The seed snatched away by the birds represented the people who heard about the kingdom of God and did not understand it. Satan came to snatch it away before they comprehended its implications for them. Those who received the message on stony places were the ones who received it gladly at first, but fell away from entrusting the message when life's difficulties came their way. Some people believed the gospel, but worldly concerns overcame their devotion to the kingdom of God and made them unfruitful. Jesus said these were the people whose faith was choked by thorns. Still other people received the seed on good ground, understood its message, and produced fruit from the seed.

Because so many other people in history longed to know the message of the kingdom of God but never got to hear it, Jesus told us to listen closely to his preaching of the gospel. In effect, Jesus told us to be like the seed that fell on good ground and produced fruit. Having heard the interpretation of the parable, Jesus equipped us to overcome the obstacles we will face to our faith becoming fruitful.

Do we hear the gospel preached, or do we not listen closely enough to understand? Do we care enough to understand, or is it like seed falling by the wayside? Do we care enough to pick it up and examine it? It is possible to completely miss the message simply because you are oblivious to it and too concerned about other things. Jesus warned us not to be this way. If we are, then the devil quickly comes to steal the good news of God's Kingdom away from us so we never get to really hear it. Satan will gladly supply something else to take its place, a distraction to capture your attention so you never really see the priceless gift landing on the ground right next to you.

A second possibility is we hear the gospel and believe its message, but difficulty and persecution cause our faith to die because we have not developed deep roots. Will we allow the gospel to take root in us? How far down into our lives are we willing to let it go? If there are rocky barriers we do not permit to be broken by the roots, then the plant of faith cannot be strongly established and a good gust of wind will blow it away. Either that or, it will grow sickly and die. If you have ever tried to grow a garden, you know plants will cease to grow if their roots are kept in a tight space like a container that is too small. They may stay alive for awhile, but will always be sickly and weak; any trouble and they quickly die.

Another possibility is we hear the word of God and it grows well in our lives. It takes root, but remains among thorny plants. These weeds eventually choke out the gospel plant and it dies. Jesus says these weeds are the "cares of this world and the deceitfulness of riches." Every single one of us has cares in this world. They are most likely different for each of us. We have families, friends, homes, cultures, hobbies, and other things people would say make up our lives. For a disciple of Jesus, however, these things do not make up our lives. We still have these aspects of life around us, but they are not our lives. Paul wrote to the Colossian believers, "Set your mind on things above, not on things on the earth. For you died and your life is hidden with Christ in God." (Colossians 3:2-3) Our life is now in Christ. That is the plant springing forth from the gospel seed. All the other cares of life, especially the attraction of riches, must not be allowed to choke out the plant God wants producing kingdom fruit in our lives. An indication of what kind of fruit Jesus intended for us to produce is found in Galatians 5:22-23.

"But the fruit of the Spirit is love, joy, peace, longsuffering, kindness, goodness, faithfulness, gentleness, and self-control."

The command of Jesus is for us to really hear what he said in this parable. He identified for us the many obstacles our faith will encounter on its way to producing the fruit of the Spirit in our lives. Armed with this knowledge, we disciples of Christ have been given a great gift, an advantage in our fight against these things. Jesus has told us the enemy's plan for making our faith unfruitful. He has warned us about three major obstacles. There is no excuse for allowing these things to overcome us since he has taken extra time to make it plain for us.

Questions:

1. If a priceless jewel landed on the ground next to you, would you pick it up? What might keep you from picking it up? Have you ever tried to tell someone the gospel and they really did not care?

2. How do worldly concerns and the "deceitfulness of riches" choke out the fruit God wants to produce in us?

3. How do deep roots keep a plant alive in adversity? What are deep roots in our life of faith?

4. What would obeying this command to "hear the parable of the sower" look like?

> *"The Son of Man will send out His angels, and they will gather out of His kingdom all things that offend, and those who practice lawlessness, and will cast them into the furnace of fire. There will be wailing and gnashing of teeth. Then the righteous will shine forth as the sun in the kingdom of their Father. He who has ears to hear, let him hear!"*
>
> —Matthew 13:41-43

Again, Jesus commands us to "hear" what he says. He is talking about the end of history as we know it. Jesus will send out angels to collect up all those who practice lawlessness and offend God. They will be thrown into Hell. People will be crying and grinding their teeth because they are not in the kingdom of God. The righteous, however, will shine brightly.

The difference between those who offend God and those who are righteous is the practice of their lives. It is what they are habitually which matters to God. Who are they really? Do they lie, cheat, and steal with impunity? Do they do these things and put a religious mask over it to conceal it from others?

"Practice" is an interesting word here. It is where we get the word "practical." This is where the kingdom of God gets down in your business. Are the practical aspects of your life operating according to God's kingdom principles? If not, look out! Jesus even uses an exclamation point at the end of his command so we get the point: hear this!

It is possible to say all the correct words about what you believe but still live your life according to the principles of the world rather than those of God. This is not a "righteous" person according to this prophecy of Jesus. The righteous person is someone who "shines forth like the sun in the kingdom of their Father." In other words, they will look like their Father; they belong in the kingdom. If you doubt this is the meaning Jesus intended, compare it with his statement at the end of the Sermon on the Mount:

"Every tree that does not bear good fruit is cut down and thrown into the fire. Therefore, by their fruits you will know them. Not everyone who says to me, 'Lord, Lord,' shall enter the kingdom of heaven, but he who does the will of my Father in heaven. Many will say to me in that day, 'Lord, Lord, have we not prophesied in your name, cast out demons in your name, and done many wonders in your name?' And then I will declare to them, 'I never knew you; depart from me, you who practice lawlessness!" (Matthew 7:19-23)

Righteous people are those who have allowed God's Spirit to bring forth God's fruit in their lives. This fruit, as described in the previous Standing Order, is not so much specific accomplishments as developed character. It is the character of God in you: "love, joy, peace, longsuffering, kindness, goodness, faithfulness, gentleness, and self-control."

Of course these people will "shine forth like the sun" when the kingdom comes. They belong there! The same radiance emanating from God comes out of them because they are made of the same character material: godliness.

Questions:

1. Does this Standing Order offend you? Why or why not?

2. How is the gospel "practical"?

3. What makes a person righteous, according to Jesus? How does this conflict with what you may have heard or thought?

4. What is the danger in assuming your outward appearance or affirming correct doctrine makes you belong in God's kingdom?

5. Why does Jesus relate all of this to a parable about sowing seed (Matthew 13:37-40)?

"They do not need to go away. You give them something to eat."

—Matthew 14:16

Jesus is about to perform a miracle by multiplying loaves of bread and fish to feed over five thousand people. He begins by issuing a command to his disciples, however. He wants them to be involved in this miracle. It is to serve not only as a provision of food, but also a lesson of faith. The lesson is this: when you encounter genuine needs in the midst of obeying God (for example, crowds of people are hungry after listening to preaching) then proceed by doing what you can to meet the need and trust God to do the rest. Jesus issued the command, "You give them something to eat."

The first reaction of the disciples is very practical. They want to send the people away so they can fend for themselves and get something to eat. Jesus was also very practical. He said they do not need to "go away" to get what they need. It was right there where they were, even though they did not see it. The disciples knew they did not have enough for all the people. Jesus said they did have enough to start. Faith does not have to be large to be effective. It simply must begin to be executed or put into practice. Faith cannot change anything when it stays inside your heart. When you choose to empty your own lunchbox and pour out your faith, that is when you will see the miracle happen.

I have seen this miracle myself once on a mission to Haiti. It was all very practical and not like a magic show at all. There were about 700-800 pastors and their families at a conference being sponsored by the local church. We were assisting the church with the logistics of the conference, feeding the people and providing tents and mattresses for sleeping. There was only one problem: we were late and most of our equipment had not arrived from the ship to the site of the conference. Our team was setting up the tents and cooking wagon, but our food supplies had not yet arrived. We only had 70 sandwiches we had packed to feed ourselves as we set up camp.

The pastors and their families came from all over the Haitian countryside, many of them walking with nothing but their Bibles in hand. They were tired and hungry, assembled under one of the tents we had managed to set up. Our chief cook came to me and asked what we were to do since there were so many hungry people and we had no cooked food to feed them. We did not even have the supplies to begin cooking yet.

Remembering Jesus' comment to the disciples, I said she should begin to cut the sandwiches into quarters and serve everyone. We could then feed about 280 people only one-quarter of a sandwich. Still, it was a beginning and it was all we had. I said, "Let's see what God will do."

Our people began passing out the sandwiches until everyone had eaten enough. Then, when we were all through, there was still a whole box of sandwiches left over! It was more than enough to feed all of our crew, also. How did this happen? I cannot explain it naturally. We did not see sandwiches magically appearing because we were too busy passing them out to notice. All I know is there is no way those sandwiches could have fed all those people, even if I had underestimated how many people were there. Also, those people were hungry and I know they were not satisfied with only a quarter of a sandwich each. They were not afraid to tell you they wanted more.

There is only one way to apprehend what happened that day in Haiti. We obeyed the command of Jesus to his disciples and he performed the same miracle he did two thousand years ago in Israel. There was no way we could have fed all of them, but then, we were doing what God asked of us and were willing to open up our lunchbox, also. This is simple obedience; it means taking Jesus at his word. There was no guarantee he was going to perform a miracle, even as he did not tell the disciples long ago what he was going to do when they shared five loaves and two fishes. But faith does not work with guarantees, it works with practical obedience to the commands of Jesus. It is a whole different way of thinking.

Once we decide to change our mind and simply obey the commands of Jesus, we should not be surprised to see many incredible things happen. This is normal in the kingdom of God! An unbelieving heart is what is abnormal. To take only the spiritual meaning of Jesus' words limits your faith to the spiritual realm, but the kingdom of God is much more than our concept of Heaven. It works itself out in very practical ways, like chicken sandwiches and loaves of bread with fish.

Questions:

1. Why would Jesus not tell his disciples he was going to perform a miracle of feeding five thousand people in advance?

2. What did his disciples have to do in order to see the miracle?

3. What does it mean when I said, "faith does not work with guarantees, it works with practical obedience to the commands of Jesus"?

4. How does this apply to other commands Jesus gave us?

5. Why is this concept of faith a "whole different way of thinking"?

"Bring them here to me."
—Matthew 14:18

"O faithless and perverse generation, how long shall I be with you? How long shall I bear with you? Bring him here to me."
—Matthew 17:17

Both of these commands precede a miracle Jesus is about to perform and they both occur when his disciples are not able to meet the need of the people. The first occurs in the context of the feeding of five thousand people with five loaves and two fishes. Jesus tells the disciples to bring the food to him first for blessing. The second command is to bring a man to Jesus whom the disciples could not heal. He had epilepsy and they prayed for him but saw no results.

Both of these commands point out an important aspect of faith. Miracles occur, not because of the size and power of our faith, but because of *who* the faith is directed towards. People will be fed not simply because they are hungry, but because they have come to hear the good news about the kingdom of God and are dependent on him to provide for their needs. Men and women will be healed not simply because of their medical need but due to their seeking after Jesus as the source of healing.

It is clear from both instances the disciples are inadequate for each task; they cannot deliver results. In each case, they are directed toward Jesus and the solution becomes apparent. In the case of the food, he allows them to be involved in the solution by beginning with what they had and passing it out. In the case of the healing, he steps in directly and heals the man.

Obedience to this command will prevent much frustration in ministry. We will inevitably come up against our human limitations when we set out to serve other people in God's name. We will not be able to meet all of their needs; in fact, we will not even get close to meeting their needs. Does that mean we should just give up? Jesus tells us to "bring them here to me."

We may not be able to feed all the people or heal all of the diseases, but we can always bring people to Jesus. We can always tell them about his love for them and go with them in prayer before God. When we do this, many times God will intervene and perform a miracle. Sometimes he will not, for unknown reasons. Still, we cannot go wrong bringing them to Jesus because it is an act of faith, a practical obedience to his command. We acknowledge our human limitation and are saying, "I cannot do this Jesus, only *you* have the power to make a difference here." He may still tell us to begin, as with the loaves and fishes, to start along in the correct direction as far as we know how. Then he will meet us there and perform the miracle. Alternatively, he may tell us to get out of the way and the person may need to come directly to him for what they need. Either way, we acknowledge him as the source to fill our lack. This is also an important aspect of faith.

Questions:

1. Have you ever felt inadequate to meet someone's need? How can you still give them what they need when you cannot provide it for them?

2. How does acknowledging our inadequacy become an opportunity for faith?

3. What aspect of faith does this command teach us?

"Be of good cheer! It is I; do not be afraid."
—Matthew 14:27

"Arise, and do not be afraid."
—Matthew 17:7

"Do not be afraid, only believe."
—Mark 5:36

"Rejoice! Do not be afraid."
—Matthew 28:9-10

Several times, Jesus commands his disciples to not be afraid. Instead, he tells them to "rejoice!" or "believe". His message shows how God wants us to feel. He does not want us to walk around being afraid of anyone or anything. Instead, he wants us to be cheerful, rejoicing people who believe their God is in control.

My personal favorite fear-alternative Jesus commands for us is in Matthew 17. The disciples have just heard a voice from heaven say Jesus is God's beloved son and they are supposed to listen to him. This is very frightening for them. Many times, people wish they heard a voice from God in the sky, but every time this happened in the Bible, the people did not seem to enjoy the experience. In both Matthew 17 and in Exodus 20, the reaction of people to hearing God speak this way was total fear. Jesus immediately tells his disciples, however, to "arise" and not be afraid. He wants them to get up after they fell on their faces in fear. God does not want us groveling on the ground at his feet like some human tyrant. He wants us to stand up and meet him as his own dear children. We can do this because of these commands Jesus gave.

Without Jesus, we would be justified in falling down before God. We do have much to fear from him apart from our relationship with his son. We are sinful, imperfect people who frequently do not display his righteousness. Jesus tells us that because he is there with us, we can arise in the presence of a holy God. We have nothing to fear with Jesus. He is with us and for us. He is the beloved son of God and we are his beloved disciples. God loves those who listen to his son.

This command to not be afraid has other implications as well. Because we are in right relationship with God, our entire life is working out alright. Are people oppressing us? Take heart, God is with us. Is there injustice in the world? Do not be afraid of the evil acts of men. Your standing with God means all will work out for you in the end. The worst anyone can do is kill you. As a disciple of Jesus, however, this is not the worst that can happen to you. You are always assured of your place with God – you *belong* to him because of your relationship with him through his son. So even if you are killed, you will be with him where you belong.

Our being with God does not begin, however, when we die. We are, rather, with him *now*, beginning the very moment we receive and believe the Gospel. So no matter what happens in life, we have the assurance of belonging with God as we pass through life and even after this life ends for us. How much energy is wasted on fear of death and scratching to live! Despite all our best attempts, we cannot prolong our lives more than what God has laid out for us to live. It is better to simply listen to Jesus on this point and not be afraid. Instead, arise, be cheerful, and rejoice in your loving relationship with God.

We accomplish this by faith. In the Gospel of Mark chapter 5, Jesus says, "Do not be afraid, only believe." He said this to a man who had reason to be afraid. People had just come to tell him his daughter had died. He had traveled a far distance to get Jesus to come and heal her, but learned he was too late. How desperate he must have felt! If only he had been a few hours earlier! Perhaps Jesus could have saved her. The news of her death threatens to smash all his hope.

There is only one way for such fear to be confronted. It is through trusting what Jesus says. It is very simple at such a point of decision. You will either trust what you see and hear and in fact know to be the facts or you will believe what God says. There is no middle ground. I call this the "cold stone wall" experience because I felt this in a very similar situation.

My pregnant wife called me with some very disturbing news at work one day. She was bleeding and believed she was miscarrying our baby. I began to pray for God to save the child's life. I can remember feeling like I was banging my head against a cold stone wall; there was no answer from heaven, no answer at all. Then I came to the realization I was either going to trust God in this matter of my child's life or I would not trust him at all. Would I trust God even if he did not save my child's life? There were only two possible answers to this question at the foot of the Cold Stone Wall. The possibilities were either "yes" or "no," there was nothing in between. I decided I would trust God no matter what happened. Our child did die that day, but my faith became stronger than steel, also. I knew no matter what happened in life, I had chosen to trust God. The other side of the Cold Stone Wall is either unbelief or complete trust in God.

Jesus is trying to help us over the Cold Stone Wall with his command to not be afraid and "only believe." Still, the choice remains ours as to which path we choose. It remains for every disciple at some point in life to make that choice. It will come in different ways for different people. It may even involve the loss of someone dear to you. Do not be afraid. Remember God loves you and has accepted you as his very own. There is great comfort in trusting him because he is trustworthy.

Questions:

1. Jesus tells us to not be afraid. How does he command we respond in place of fear?

2. Why does it make sense to not be afraid when there are so many real reasons to fear in life? Is it naïve to obey this command?

3. What basis do we have as disciples of Jesus to not be afraid of God?

4. What is the challenge of the Cold Stone Wall? Have you ever experienced something similar? If not, what would be such a scenario for you?

5. What happens on the other side of the Cold Stone Wall? What happened for the man in Mark chapter 5? What happened for me?

"Come."

—Matthew 14:29

Jesus gives this command to Peter after he has confronted the fear of seeing Jesus walking on the water. Peter obeyed the command of Jesus to "be of good cheer" and not be afraid. In fact, he is so excited about seeing Jesus walking on the water he wants to walk out there with him! This brings an interesting response from Jesus. He issues another command: "Come."

This command follows obedience to the first. It requires trust in Jesus to even get this command to "come." In effect, Jesus is telling Peter to do something impossible. He could not walk on the water any more than you or I can today! So far, Peter has shown his faith by obeying a command Jesus has given. So Jesus gives him something even more impossible to believe.

God will often follow up a first step of faith with another more ludicrous leap. It is as if he is drawing out your faith to see how far you are willing to go. In this case, Peter got out of the boat and actually walked out to Jesus. Then he got distracted by the fact he was doing the impossible and began to be afraid. He went back into fear. Then he cried out to Jesus to save him as he sank.

Jesus did not scold him for this. He simply said, "Oh you of little faith, why did you doubt?" (Matthew 14:31) as he caught Peter's hand. He asked him a question. If you believed me before, Peter, and you were not afraid, why did you become afraid once you realized you were doing the impossible? Even a little bit of faith had Peter out walking on the water while the other eleven disciples were still scared in the boat. It is as if Jesus showed him how his obedience to the first command to "not be afraid" enabled him to do the impossible. When his doubt overcame his trust, this was the point of failure. It is always the point of failure for us, too.

When we begin to follow Jesus, we will see amazing things begin to happen, even miracles. This is normal life in the kingdom of God. It is a wild ride following Jesus. He will take you places you never would have gone and you will do things you never would have dreamed of doing. Still, you will look around yourself sometime and think, "How did I get out here?" It will seem to be a long way from safety. When you give in to the fear and doubt, you will begin to sink, just like Peter. None of us has perfect faith like Jesus. Still, when we get excited about obeying him and rejoice in doing his will, it seems to overcome our lingering doubts and we step "out of the boat." When we do begin to sink, however, Jesus is right there to save us. He will not let us go down.

Never be ashamed of stepping out and failing. Remember, Peter at least walked on the water. The others were too scared to set foot out of the boat. Peter experienced something no one else in history had done. You will have similar experiences as you follow Jesus. Your failures are surpassed by the accomplishment of faith. To receive the command to "Come" is a high honor. It means you have passed beyond the basic level of simply not being afraid and are now operating on the level of going where Jesus is, doing what Jesus is doing. When we lay down our fear and trust Jesus, each of us will receive a similar command to "Come." Do not look down or around, just get up and go!

Questions:

1. How is the command to "Come" a follow up to the command not to be afraid?

2. How did the excitement and joy of seeing Jesus help Peter move beyond fear of the circumstances?

3. What did Jesus want from Peter after he overcame fear?

4. Where is our "point of failure"?

5. Why should we not be ashamed of failing after we trusted God?

> *"Hear and understand: not what goes into the mouth defiles a man; but what comes out of the mouth, this defiles a man."*
>
> —Matthew 15:11

Again, Jesus commanded us to "hear and understand" something. He wanted his disciples to listen and let the implications of his teaching really sink into their minds. The ceremonial requirements of religion according to the Law of Moses forbid the eating of certain foods. If one ate these foods, one was considered ceremonially unclean, not properly fit to be in the presence of God for worship. Leviticus chapter 11 provides the laws of which animals are clean and unclean. It is a long list. In fact, if someone so much as touched one of these unclean animals, he was considered unclean all day and he was required to wash his clothes.

This is all clearly laid out in the Law. Then along comes Jesus and makes a very subversive statement. This is the statement he has commanded us to "hear and understand." He says not the foods you eat defile you, but rather what you say. The words from your mouth are what can make you unacceptable to come into the presence of God. Unwholesome and unclean words are what require "washing," not our clothes.

This is a radical departure from religious practice. It is a complete turning on its head of the idea religious life is adherence to a set of rules. Instead, Jesus is saying true religious life is who you *are* inside. What sort of heart do you have? For, as he says later in the same chapter of Matthew, "those things which proceed out of the mouth come from the heart and they defile a man."

Each of us is given a window into what is in our hearts if we would listen to what we say. There we could clearly hear the evil thoughts, judgment, lies, and blasphemies. What we need is not rules, but a new heart. This makes clear Jesus' statement elsewhere to Nicodemus, "You must be born again." (John 3:7) In fact, Jesus said it is impossible for anyone to even *see* the kingdom of God without being born again. (John 3:3) Anyone who thinks the kingdom of God is about following religious rules has completely missed it. Jesus corrected this misperception and commanded us to "hear and understand."

Nothing could be more important for disciples of Jesus than seeing the kingdom of God. It is alive and spreading out in every time and every place, not just thousands of years ago when Jesus was walking the earth. Can you see the kingdom of God today? If not, you may be looking in the wrong place. It is found inside your heart, not religious ceremonies, even good ones prescribed by the Bible. God's kingdom is expanding because more hearts are being changed to become more and more like him.

Questions:

1. What did Jesus want us to "hear and understand"?

2. Why can food not defile a person according to Jesus?

3. Why do words show a person to be "unclean"?

4. Why is it so important to be "born again" in Jesus' opinion?

5. How does this command to understand what makes a person unclean help you understand what it means to be "born again"?

> *"Let them alone. They are blind leaders of the blind. And if the blind leads the blind, both will fall into a ditch."*
> —Matthew 15:14

Jesus had a command for his disciples regarding their relations with the Pharisees. He said, "Let them alone." In other words, do not have anything to do with them. He calls them "blind leaders of the blind." They do not know where they are going. Their problem is they *think* they are leading people to God, but instead are taking them in another direction.

It is curious how Jesus wants his disciples to deal with religious leaders more concerned about rules than character. He wants us to ignore them. He did not say the disciples should argue with them or try to take religious positions of authority from them. "Let them alone," is his answer. It can seem incredibly naïve to obey this command. You mean we should just let people like that go on teaching and preaching such false doctrines? But what about the people they are deceiving?

Jesus clearly does not want his disciples involved in struggles for power or authority. He wants them to have a proper understanding of what the kingdom of God is and to teach this understanding to others. So much effort can be wasted in political maneuvering to get the upper hand. This is how the world works. Politics is used to impose an agenda upon others. Each party, whether political or religious, decides what is most important and then works hard at displacing the other to bring its agenda as the priorities for the group.

Jesus ignored all this maneuvering. He did not attempt to stage a reform movement within Judaism by getting himself or his disciples elected to the ruling council. He did not try to displace Rome as the governing authority on the world stage.

He simply walked around telling people the truth about God and his kingdom. This is what he also expected of his disciples and what he expects of us as well. We would do well to heed this Standing Order to "Let them alone." If we do not, we waste our time on political and religious struggles which have no bearing on the kingdom of God.

There are many other commands Jesus left for us which spell out exactly what we *are* supposed to be doing. This one tells us how we should *not* spend our time. By focusing on clearly teaching and preaching the Gospel of the kingdom of God, we are using God's methods to bring about God's kingdom. We do what Jesus did, focusing on his priorities. This is how people can become "born again," which Jesus said is a requirement for being able to see the kingdom of God.

Questions:

1. Why would Jesus tell his disciples to leave the Pharisees alone?

2. What does this say about his view of religious power and authority?

3. What are Jesus' priorities?

4. How does this command impact your view of religious institutions and denominations?

"Take heed and beware of the leaven of the Pharisees and the Sadducees."
—Matthew 16:6

"Beware of the leaven of the Pharisees, which is hypocrisy."
—Luke 12:1

"Beware of the scribes, who love to go around in long robes in the marketplaces, the best seats in the synagogues, and the best places at feasts, who devour widow's houses, and for a pretense make long prayers. These will receive greater condemnation."
—Luke 20:46-47

"Take heed, beware of the leaven of the Pharisees and the leaven of Herod."
—Mark 8:15

"Woe to you, scribes and Pharisees, hypocrites! For you pay tithe of mint and anise and cumin, and have neglected the weightier matters of the law; justice and mercy and faith. These you ought to have done without leaving the others undone."
—Matthew 23:23

"First cleanse the inside of the cup and dish, that the outside may be clean also."
—Matthew 23:26

"Beware of the scribes, who desire to go around in long robes, love greetings in the marketplaces, the best seats in

the synagogues, and the best places at feasts, who devour widow's houses, and for a pretense, make long prayers. These will receive greater condemnation."
—Mark 12:38-40

In the last Standing Order, Jesus commanded his disciples to leave the Pharisees alone. This next Standing Order is to "Take heed, beware" of the scribes and Pharisees and Jesus tells us why: hypocrisy. He identifies this as the greatest sin of the religious people and the reason why his disciples should beware of them.

Such people are caught up in the rules and regulations of religion. They love the ceremonies and feasts, titles and recognition, power and authority given to them because of their religious positions. By focusing on these aspects of religion, Jesus says they had forgotten what the kingdom of God is all about: "justice and mercy and faith." Again, these are character traits of God. This is what the kingdom of God is all about, developing the character of God in our hearts, his way of thinking and being. The religious leaders tended to focus on the outward appearances of religion instead. It is still a temptation for religious leaders today. Perhaps this is because it is so much easier to track and keep account of outward religious obligations. Internal character development requires actual relationship and relationships can be messy.

Jesus had a reason for issuing this Standing Order. He did not want his disciples to get caught up in religious hypocrisy. This means it is a real threat. The Pharisees were not bad people. In fact, they thought they were following God's Law to the letter as best they could. They thought this made them a "cut above" other people because of their strict obedience to God. In striving to obey the Standing Orders of Jesus, this Order is particularly important because it keeps us from falling into the same trap. It reminds us to always beware of potential hypocrisy in ourselves. Do we profess God's ways and then conveniently forget to apply them to ourselves? Do we focus on the outward signs of obedience and forget to develop the fruit of the Spirit in our lives? Do we glory in the public benefits of religious power? Such dangers are real and Jesus wants his disciples to be fully aware of the pitfalls and avoid them.

Questions:

1. What was the sin of the scribes and Pharisees about which Jesus warned his disciples?

2. How is this sin a trap for people serious about obeying God?

3. How does this sin impede the progress of the Kingdom of God?

4. Jesus said people like the scribes and Pharisees would "receive greater condemnation." What do you think this means?

5. How does this Standing Order help a disciple of Jesus?

> *"If anyone desires to come after me, let him deny himself, take up his cross, and follow me."*
> —Matthew 16:24

Jesus gives three straightforward commands to anyone who wants to be his disciple, to "come after" him. First, he says, "let him deny himself." This is the beginning of following in the footsteps of Jesus. It all begins with denying your own will and accepting the will of God for your life.

We all have some idea of what our life should look like, what we want it to look like, what we wish it would look like. These ideas are not necessarily God's ideas. Jesus must have had his own ideas what his life could have been like. Perhaps he would have married or managed a carpentry business. Maybe a quiet little life awaited him in northern Israel, far away from the religious and political controversies of the Pharisees and Rome. Even better, he could have religious disciples and teach them the Law as so many Jewish rabbis before him had done. His interpretations could have been esteemed by all Israel and he could have been a well-respected teacher like Gamaliel of the Sanhedrin.

This was not God's will for Jesus. His plan for this incredibly gifted man involved a cross, public humiliation, and death. In order for Jesus to fulfill God's will, he had to confront this future. In fact, we see him in the process of confronting this fact in the Garden of Gethsemane, "My soul is overwhelmed with sorrow to the point of death….My Father, if it is possible, may this cup be taken from me. Yet not as I will, but as you will." (Mathew 26:38-39).

The first step for the disciple of Jesus is to deny his will for himself. The second takes him where Jesus himself went, for he tells the disciple to "take up his cross." Jesus carried his cross on the way to his own execution. Taking up our cross is, in a sense, to carry the method of our own execution willingly. A cross is a very public and humiliating way to die. You hang there for everyone to see until you cannot breathe any longer. Once you cannot draw any more breath, you expire in full view of everyone who cares to watch. You are completely helpless. For a disciple to "take up his cross", he must realize it is his own death he is carrying, not that of Jesus.

Jesus died on his cross in order to defeat sin and death by his resurrection. He commands his disciples to take up their own crosses, their own executions and humiliations so they too can be raised in Resurrection life. This involves an intense faith in God because there is no guarantee you will emerge on the other side of death except for God's promise to you. Every fiber of your natural being is tuned to survival and will resist you taking up this cross of execution. In each case, the cross will look different because each disciple is different. One commonality, however, is the cross will look and feel like death to you; death of your dreams, your identity and vision of life.

The other side of the cross is the last part of this command: "follow me." We can see only one thing beyond the cross we take up. It is Jesus on the other side, beckoning us to follow. He has gone before us to show the way. We are not left on our own to figure it out ourselves. Paul tells us in his letter to the Romans, "For those God foreknew he also predestined to be conformed to the likeness of his Son, that he might be the firstborn among many brothers." (Romans 8:29) God's will is for us to be formed in the image of Jesus. He bore his cross; we must carry ours. It helps to know on the other side of our cross, however, is God's ultimate goal for us. The cross is not the goal, it is the pathway toward the goal of becoming like Christ. It is a door through which Christ himself stepped and now wants us to step through so we can be with him.

There is only one promise given to us on this side of our cross, before we carry it. The promise is when we take it up, it is God's will for us to accomplish his purpose of making us like his Son. He wants to populate heaven with people who are like Jesus. So while our cross represents very real death and loss, even humiliation, it is also the only way forward if we want to follow Jesus. Every disciple faces this fact just as Jesus did.

A much more comforting fact is we will be with Jesus once we take up our cross. He not only went before us, he is there *with* us, encouraging us, wanting us to succeed. He loves it when people take it up because it means they will be with him. We can love it too, even as we watch our dreams die or our vision of our life disappear because we know we will be <u>with Jesus</u>. This is our comfort and the very great reward of every disciple of Jesus.

Questions:

1. What does it mean for a disciple of Jesus to "deny himself"?

2. What is a "cross" Jesus says disciples must "take up"? What could possibly be your cross?

3. Why is a cross necessary for every disciple to follow Jesus?

4. Do we have any guarantees from God about what life will be like once we begin to walk with our cross?

"Assuredly, I say to you, unless you are converted and become as little children, you will by no means enter the kingdom of heaven."
—Matthew 8:3

"Let the little children come to me and do not forbid them; for of such is the kingdom of heaven."
—Matthew 19:14

"Take heed that you do not despise one of these little ones, for I say to you that in heaven their angels always see the face of my Father who is in heaven."
—Matthew 18:10

"Whoever receives one of these little children in my name receives me; and whoever receives me receives not me, but Him who sent me."
—Mark 9:37

Jesus has very specific ideas about children. Our tendency as adults is to make children like us. We view it as our job to civilize them and train them up to be good citizens of the culture to which we belong. Jesus, however, assures us we cannot even enter the kingdom of heaven unless we become like little children. He says we must "be converted" – in other words, our hearts must be changed.

This heart change involves a peculiar characteristic of little children. They implicitly trust people and the world around them. They are not suspicious or cynical, thinking they know better. Only as they develop and become trained by adults do they begin to think they know something and have the qualifications to interpret what they see around them. Little children simply accept the world as they experience it.

In the same way, Jesus wants us to accept God as He is, accept His authority and Creation the way He made it, not as we would like to fashion it. No child ever argued a theological point with Jesus, only adult Pharisees. Children never doubted his ability to heal or his attraction as Messiah. They just came to him when their parents brought them. They accepted Jesus as he was and they realized they wanted to be with him.

Jesus gives his disciples a strict warning not to prevent children from coming to him. Adults tend to think Jesus is too important to be bothered with children, their presence is somehow embarrassing. Children ask too many questions and talk about subjects adults have been trained to avoid. Their simplicity and directness are qualities Jesus wants his disciples to emulate. His command is simple: do not forbid children to come near him. This applied to his bodily presence in Israel and it applies to his spiritual presence among the Church. Disciples of Jesus must not prevent children from coming into the presence of God. Do not separate them into sterile babysitting rooms so the adults can enjoy worship. Do not think because they cannot understand God their presence among the gathered people of God is useless. Wherever Jesus is, bring them, just like the parents did long ago.

Jesus also tells us not to despise little children. Do not think of yourself as better or above them. He assures us in heaven, they have angels watching out for them and these angels are in the presence of God on their behalf. This should change our opinion of how God views children! It means He is constantly aware of their presence, attentive to their needs. He has assigned special agents to advocate for the children 24 hours a day, 7 days a week. Jesus is turning our adult view of children upside-down. They are very valuable to God, not just because they are cute, or they are future adults. He views their childhood innocence as an example for us to follow.

In order not to be misunderstood, Jesus makes an incredible statement. He says, "whoever receives one of these little children in my name receives me." Jesus equates the way we receive little children with the way we receive him. So if we are arrogant toward them, we are acting arrogant toward him. If we ignore them, we ignore him. If we think they are a nuisance, we are saying Jesus is bothersome to us. This should cause us to pause a bit and evaluate how we think about little children, if we consider ourselves to be disciples of Jesus. It certainly must have made Peter and the other disciples stop telling parents to keep the kids away or quiet. Jesus' command about children changes not just our behavior toward them but our attitude about them. We begin to value them and their qualities we thought were annoying and unsophisticated. The reason Jesus wants this change is these qualities are attributes of Kingdom citizens, disciples of Jesus Christ.

Questions:

1. What does Jesus mean when he says we must be "converted" to become like little children?

2. Why does he say this conversion is so important?

3. What qualities of little children fit descriptions of Kingdom citizens found elsewhere in the teaching of Jesus?

4. How does God show He thinks children are important?

5. What would change in your life and your church if you had this attitude toward children?

"If your hand or foot causes you to sin, cut it off and cast it from you."

—Matthew 18:8

Jesus prescribes a simple remedy for things in our lives that cause us to sin. He says we should cut them off and throw them away. The image he uses of amputating a hand or foot conveys the urgency of this command. No matter how dear something is to you, how necessary it seems to your life, if it causes you to sin against God or your neighbor, cut it off and throw it away. This ensures it will not be nearby to tempt you in the future. Jesus is making a statement about the relative importance of such things compared with your eternal life. Nothing is worth risking hellfire for eternity, no sin is to be tolerated.

Implicit in this statement is an awareness of sin in your life. If you are not aware of sin, then you will not know certain things are causing you to sin. For example, a man may think viewing pornography is a harmless habit; it simply satisfies his craving for sexual stimulation. No one seems hurt by it because it only occurs in complete privacy. The action of God's spirit in our lives, however, brings awareness to sin. The man begins to see how the pornography provokes lust in his soul. He sees how it colors his relationships with the women in his life and how it affects his views of women he does not even know. He may become aware it creates a barrier between himself and God; he realizes it is sinful.

Now, if the man stops looking at pornography but retains it, keeps his access to it, the desire for viewing pornography will quickly overcome his desire to clean up his life. The lust for pornography will torment him until he gives in to the desire. He will be a very miserable disciple of Jesus, knowing he is in sin and yet unable to overcome its power. Jesus gave this command to provide strong medicine for sin and its power. By cutting it off and casting it from him, the man enslaved to pornography is free from its power. It is better for him to live without sexual stimulation than to be constantly tormented.

Some people may say it would be better then to simply deny there is any such thing as sin. You could avoid the whole painful process of dealing with "cutting off your hand." You could be a Christian by going to church, believing Jesus died so you are completely forgiven for all your mistakes, and then go on happily with your life. You could simply accept the sin as part of your nature, something which will change when Jesus comes back, but requires no superhuman efforts to overcome. This is a very dangerous and risky path.

Jesus tells us plainly, "Woe to the world because of the things that cause people to sin! Such things must come, but woe to the man through whom they come!….It is better for you to enter life maimed or crippled than to have two hands or two feet and be thrown into eternal fire." (Matthew 18:7-8) He pronounces woe will come, great suffering and hardship, even eternal fire. This eternal judgment is upon all sin. Our awareness of sin demands a response to it: we must get rid of its source. The alternative is unthinkable for a disciple – eternal hell. One might be tempted to think Jesus is only talking about the world here, not his disciples. He makes it very clear he means *everyone* by saying to his disciples, "It is better for *you* to enter into life maimed or crippled than to have two hands or two feet and be thrown into eternal fire." Even his disciples are playing with fire when they play with sin.

Do not play with sin; instead, cut it off and throw it away as Jesus commanded. This will save you much pain. According to his words, the pain awaits you even if you are ignorant of or choose to ignore the sin. It is a blessing God reveals our sin to us so we can do something about it with his help.

Questions:

1. Why would Jesus talk about cutting off hands and feet when he is speaking about removing sin from your life?

2. Why is it unwise to deny sin exists or ignore it in your life when God makes you aware of it?

3. What is the purpose of Jesus commanding his disciples to get rid of things causing them to sin? What is his ultimate goal in doing this?

4. Why are you playing with fire when you play with sin?

5. When you obey this command of Jesus, what are you saying is more valuable to you than whatever sin has become so dear or comfortable?

"If your brother sins against you, go and tell him his fault between you and him alone. If he hears you, you have gained your brother. But if he will not hear, take with you one or two more, that 'by the mouth of two or three witnesses every word may be established.' And if he refuses to hear them, tell it to the church. But if he refuses even to hear the church, let him be to you like a heathen and tax collector."

—Matthew 18:15-17

At Friend Ships, a ministry I served with, we agreed to a Code of Conduct that contains this rule Jesus commands. He said to go to who sins against you and tell him, just between the two of you. We are not to involve anyone else in the dispute. Our first day at Friend Ships, we read the Code of Conduct and sign a paper promising to live by the community rules. Part of my job as one of the directors at Friend Ships was to explain the Code of Conduct to new crew and answer any questions they asked. I have met with hundreds of people and not a single one has ever disagreed with this command of Jesus.

Another part of my job was to remind people what the Code of Conduct says when they encountered interpersonal difficulties. So I have had the opportunity to see how dedicated Christians actually handle interpersonal conflict. Surprisingly, the same people who agree with Jesus' command at the beginning seem to encounter a selective amnesia when it comes down to applying it to themselves later.

It is much easier to talk with someone else about an offense than it is to go to the offending party and tell them what they have done to you. Even if the offender is approached, it is rare to see them approached with an attitude of love, with the objective of "gaining your brother." Usually the offended person will react in anger, tell the other person off, and cause even greater interpersonal conflict.

Jesus gives us not only really good advice for resolving conflict, but a command he expects us to obey. If this method were used consistently, I am confident 99% of all interpersonal conflicts in churches would be solved immediately. Sadly, this does not happen. Instead, we give the devil room to enter our relationships because of our disobedience to Jesus. Once the conflict spreads to involve more than one person, it becomes a family problem.

There are cases, however, when the disputing parties cannot work out their problems. Jesus is aware of this and provides for it in his command. The offended person is to take one or two witnesses from the church family to approach the offender. This is an attempt to resolve the dispute within the family, but minimizing the impact of the dispute on the whole family. These witnesses are not resolving the conflict for the two parties. They are simply there to observe how the attempt at resolution is progressing and in what manner the attempt is made. They may restate the case of the offended person so the offender has the opportunity to hear it from someone else. He may realize what he has done and apologize.

Following these two steps should resolve 99.9% of all interpersonal conflicts among disciples of Jesus. Sometimes, however, people can be stubborn. In this case, the problem is to be taken to the whole church, the leaders and decision-makers in the local assembly of disciples. If the offender refuses to heed them, Jesus commands us to treat him as the Jews would a heathen or tax collector. In other words, have nothing to do with him. The hope throughout this whole process is the offender will come to his senses and see his mistake. The goal is always to restore him to proper relationship with the offended person and with the rest of the church. In the case of the hard-hearted person, who refuses to hear the witnesses or leaders of the church, he has separated himself from the community because of his intransigence. Treating him like a tax collector would be entirely justified, just as Jesus said.

If Jesus' procedure is followed carefully, the Holy Spirit works to resolve conflicts among disciples. He enjoys doing this – he *wants* to do this. You will find it much easier to work things out when you follow this command simply because you are obeying Jesus.

Questions:

1. How many church conflicts could be quickly resolved if this command of Jesus was obeyed?

2. What happens when you discuss interpersonal problems with a third person without talking to the offender privately?

3. What is the goal of the confrontations Jesus outlines in this command? Does it imply a certain attitude to have when the person is confronted?

4. Why is it easy to agree with Jesus in theory, but difficult to actually practice this command?

"Whoever desires to be first among you, let him be your slave."
—Matthew 20:27

"Whoever of you desires to be first shall be slave of all."
—Mark 10:44

"The kings of the Gentiles exercise lordship over them, and those who exercise authority over them are called 'benefactors.' But not so among you; on the contrary, he who is greatest among you, let him be as the younger, and he who governs as he who serves."
—Luke 22:25-26

"If I then, your Lord and Teacher, have washed your feet, you also ought to wash one another's feet."
—John 13:14

Here is the concept popularly known as "servant leadership." Except with Jesus, it is not a concept, it is a command. He expects leaders among his disciples will act this way. They will be servants because they have already had the attitude of a servant before they even became leaders. The first instance of this command is worded, "whoever desires to be first among you…." This means Jesus is addressing people who are not first yet. He is giving this command to all of his disciples, not just potential leaders. When a disciple becomes a leader, he should already have this character quality.

To help show the difference between his disciples and world leaders, he explained "the kings of the Gentiles exercise lordship….but not so among you." Leadership in the kingdom of God is based on the character of God, not human example. Jesus showed his respect for the attitude of little children by telling his disciples they must become like them in order to enter the kingdom of God. In this command, he says the greatest among his disciples should be like the youngest; in other words, like those least esteemed. He who governs should be like those who serve.

What is the attitude of a servant? First, the servant realizes he is not in charge. He is simply there to execute the orders of his master. In the kingdom of God, there is only one master: God himself. There is only one person with ultimate authority: God's son Jesus. The servant who finds himself in a leadership position must always remember this point. The people he leads, the community for which he is responsible belongs to someone else. He has been asked to care for it.

Second, a servant will not only do exactly what his master wishes, but also attempts to know what his master prefers. This way, the servant can do what he knows his master would want even when he has no specific instruction from the master. A servant is well-acquainted with his master's will. Every disciple given a position of leadership or authority over other disciples of Jesus must make every effort to know the mind of God. He must become intimate with God's way of thinking so he can do what is pleasing to God. Jesus himself provided an example. "When you have lifted up the Son of Man, then you will know that I am the one I claim to be and that I do nothing on my own but speak just what the Father has taught me. The one who sent me is with me; he has not left me alone, for I always do what pleases him." (John 8:28-29) Jesus did nothing on his own, because he learned what pleases the Father and did those things.

His example gives extra emphasis to this command because he specifically said, "If I then, your Lord and Teacher, have washed your feet, you also ought to wash one another's feet." (John 13:14) Since I, your master, have performed the duties of a servant to you by washing your feet, you must also do the same. The command carries extra force because Jesus himself did it and this was clearly unexpected and even a reversal of what was expected. We would expect the youngest or lowliest person would have been assigned such a menial task. Jesus says the leaders should jump to perform those tasks in his kingdom. If they have been serving long before they were ever in a position of leadership, this will be easy for them, they will be used to it. If, however, they follow the example of the world, they will expect all the perks and privileges awarded to a Chief Executive Officer. Those who start serving now will be well prepared for leadership when the time comes, confident they are obeying the ultimate master in the kingdom of God.

Questions:

1. Why is it important for potential leaders in God's kingdom to be servants before they are put in positions of leadership?

2. What are the three aspects of a servant attitude?

3. Some business management consultants teach "servant leadership" as a successful business model. This is based on the fact it can be very effective. What makes a servant attitude important for Kingdom service? What if having the attitude of a servant was not effective management in a certain situation?

"Render therefore to Caesar the things that are Caesar's and to God the things that are God's."
—Matthew 22:21

"Render to Caesar the things that are Caesar's and to God the things that are God's."
—Mark 12:17

"Render therefore to Caesar the things that are Caesar's and to God the things that are God's."
—Luke 20:25

"The scribes and the Pharisees sit in Moses' seat. Therefore, whatever they tell you to observe, that observe and do, but do not do according to their works; for they say, and do not do."
—Matthew 23:2-3

As disciples of Jesus, we are given fairly plain instructions how we are to relate with civil and religious authority. The basic question the Pharisees attempted to trick Jesus with was about whether a follower of God should pay taxes to the government (Caesar). To understand this properly, it is important to understand Caesar's government was not democratically elected and it was not kind to non-citizens. Roman governors were appointed over conquered territories and the interests of Rome were maintained by the Roman legions. People were required to pay taxes to the Roman government even though they had no voice in government.

The Roman government could not in any way be called godly. It was very religious because it allowed a place for public worship of any pagan god you could imagine. The Jewish religion was tolerated by Rome and allowed to practice, but the Jews had to subsidize the pagan government with their taxes. This meant their money was used to fund the Roman legions that sometimes treated their people like dogs. It also meant their money funded official pagan sacrifices and the building of temples to false gods. Surely, God would not blame anyone who refused to pay taxes to such a brutal and pagan government? This was the answer they were hoping to receive from Jesus so they would have grounds to accuse him before the Roman authorities.

Jesus gave an entirely different view. By commanding us to "render to Caesar the things that are Caesar's" Jesus told us to give what belongs to the civil authority what rightfully belongs to it. The government issues money. Caesar's head was on the coin. If you are participating in the government's economy, then you must pay taxes to the government. By using Caesar's money, you are subjecting yourself in some way to Caesar voluntarily. Notice, however, Jesus avoided giving a blanket statement of support for the government. He limited what we owe the civil authority to what we have implicitly agreed to owe by our own voluntary participation in its systems.

If you use roads, you will be expected to pay taxes on the roads. It is difficult to imagine how one could ever be completely independent of the civil authority's systems. In whatever way we do participate in them, Jesus is saying we must pay our dues. Disciples of Jesus are not freeloaders. They are citizens of the Kingdom of God residing in a foreign land. As such, they represent God's kingdom and its values. One of those values is personal responsibility. Paul wrote to the Thessalonian disciples, "Make it your ambition to lead a quiet life, to mind your own business and to work with your hands, just as we told you, so that your daily life may win the respect of outsiders and so that you will not be dependent on anybody." (1 Thessalonians 4:11-12) Disciples of Christ look after their own affairs and earn their way so they are not dependent on anybody. Because of this, we should be mindful of our responsibility to the civil authority while at the same time minimizing our dependence on it.

Jesus gives a wonderful example of this principle when Peter is approached by the Temple tax collectors and asked if his master paid the tax. Herod's Temple was a religious building, but it was also a massive public works project requiring large amounts of funding from tax revenue. This is why there were such amazing carved stones and columns so impressive to Jesus' disciples (Mark 13:1-2). No expense was spared on the building of Herod's Temple; it was the public legacy of a king who wanted to be remembered as "Herod the Great." Peter told the tax collectors Jesus did pay the tax. Jesus then asked him, "What do you think, Simon? From whom do the kings of the earth collect duty and taxes – from their own sons or from others?"

"From others," Peter answered.

"Then the sons are exempt," Jesus said to him. "But so that we may not offend them, go to the lake and throw out your line. Take the first fish you catch; open its mouth and you will find a four-drachma coin. Take it and give it to them for my tax and yours." (Matthew 17:25-26)

The point Jesus made was the sons of God are not required by God to pay taxes to him. They do not have an obligation to him in this way. However, the civil and religious authorities levied the tax on everyone in Israel to pay for the Temple. Jesus and his disciples used the Temple space quite often in his teaching ministry and for prayer. It is interesting Jesus took responsibility for paying this tax even though he demonstrated he and his disciples had no actual obligation to do so from God's perspective. He did not want to offend the authorities over something as trivial as paying two coins. Certainly, Jesus was not afraid of offending the religious and civil authorities; he did it quite frequently!

He makes his point the sons of God are not dependent on the civil and religious system of the authorities by telling Peter to go throw his line out for a fish. The provision of the money for the tax is made through the natural world, God's Creation. Incredibly, inside the fish's mouth is enough money to pay for both Peter and Jesus! It is as if Jesus said, "Ha! Is that the best you can do – collect money? God's provision for his children is unlimited!"

The second part of Jesus' response to the Pharisees is just as important as the first: "Render to Caesar the things that are Caesar's and to God the things that are God's." While Caesar may have some claim to our money, God has claim to our ultimate allegiance and dependence. Our Father in heaven is the one we depend on for what we need, even to the extent if you demand money from us, He is able to provide for us from the mouth of a fish! It is important to remember while Jesus is not a political rebel, he is also not a government booster. His allegiance is with God the Father, his dependence is on Him. It is the same for every disciple of Jesus.

In addition to the civil authority, Jesus also encountered the religious authorities. These were duly appointed leaders of God's people. The problem was many were also corrupt hypocrites. How does a disciple of Jesus deal with them? Jesus gave specific instructions: "whatever they tell you to observe, that observe and do, but do not do according to their works; for they say, and do not do." (Matthew 23:2-3) He does not tell his disciples to form rival factions and challenge the religious authorities for power. He does not tell them to leave the synagogue and form a separate group. Instead, he told his disciples to do what the religious leaders say, but not do what they do. In other words, follow their orders about religious observance and ceremonies in worship, but do not be a hypocrite like them.

If they require you to tithe, do it with an attitude of generosity. When they tell you to attend a religious ceremony, do it in worship of God. But when they try to make you like themselves, remember God is making you in the image of Jesus, not anyone else. Jesus told them, "Woe to you, teachers of the law and Pharisees, you hypocrites! You travel over land and sea to win a single convert, and when he becomes one, you make him twice as much a son of hell as you are." (Matthew 23:15) Corrupt religious leaders may "sit in Moses' seat," or be duly appointed authorities, but do not allow them to make you like them, sons of hell. Instead, perform your duties and keep your heart following Jesus.

Whether speaking about civil or religious authority, Jesus made it clear the ultimate allegiance of his disciples is to God. He encouraged them to fulfill their obligations, but to always remember being his disciples makes us spiritually free. Neither the government nor religious leaders have the final word; God does.

Questions:

1. In what ways is Jesus' command about how we relate to authorities supportive of them?

2. In what ways is Jesus' command subversive of authority?

3. Why would Jesus tell us to observe everything corrupt religious leaders tell us to do?

4. Why is it important for disciples of Jesus to pay taxes to the government?

5. How does this command paint a picture of how Jesus views the Kingdom of God in relation to authority on earth?

"You shall love the Lord your God with all your heart, with all your soul, and with all your mind."
—Matthew 22:37

"You shall love your neighbor as yourself."
—Matthew 22:39

"The first of all the commandments is: 'Hear O Israel, the Lord our God, the Lord is one. And you shall love the Lord your God with all your heart, with all your soul, with all your mind, and with all your strength.' This is the first commandment. And the second, like it, is this: 'You shall love your neighbor as yourself.' There is no other commandment greater than these."
—Mark 12:29-31

"Do this and you will live....Go and do likewise."
—Luke 10:28,37

The Old Testament is a valuable resource in the Bible not only because of the rich history, poetry, and wisdom found therein, but also because it contains the Law of God. The Law is a window into what God is like. It sets in simple terms for the Hebrew nation how it should worship this God who delivered them from Egypt. They had lived in Egypt for 400 years and were exposed to many ideas about how to worship the gods of Egypt. The God of Abraham, Isaac, and Jacob, however, is totally different than the Egyptian deities. Because of this difference, the Hebrews needed a Law to show them how He expected them to be different, how they could act in a way pleasing to Him.

God, in fact, wrote the covenant of the Law himself on two stone tablets for Moses (Exodus 31:18). Even as God wrote the covenant in stone for Moses, Jesus summarized it for his disciples with two commands: love God with your whole heart and love your neighbor as yourself. Jesus said no other command is greater than these in the whole Law. In effect, Jesus told us how to live according to the Law by fulfilling these commands.

When an expert in the Law questioned Jesus about how to inherit eternal life, Jesus asked the expert what he thought the Law said. The expert summarized the Law essentially just as Jesus did: love God and love your neighbor. He also wanted to justify himself, so he asked, "Who is my neighbor?" At this, Jesus told the famous parable of the Good Samaritan. (Luke 10:30-36) Then Jesus asked the expert who in the story was a neighbor to the injured man. The expert answered correctly, it was the Samaritan who had shown mercy. Jesus then responded with another command, "Go and do likewise."

Essentially, Jesus interprets the Law for us as an attitude of love, both towards God and even strangers. This love is prioritized for us: love God first and then love others in the same way you love yourself. This priority is important, because it is not God's will that loving others should ever come between him and his disciples. Loving God is not up for negotiation and we cannot allow ourselves to be manipulated by other people into putting them before him. We are encouraged to put others and their needs before ourselves if they need mercy. The priest and the Levite who walked by the Samaritan on the road probably had very good reasons why they could not stop to help him. The Law did not permit them to handle dead bodies, it would defile them and prevent them from performing their religious duties (Leviticus 21:1). Every good reason, even lawful reasons, are trumped by the attitude of mercy. Jesus sets this up as the true expression of love God communicated in the Law. This is exactly why Jesus scolded the Pharisees and scribes, saying they strained out a gnat but swallowed a camel (Matthew 23:23-24).

In answer to the lawyer's question about attaining eternal life, Jesus did not tell him to pray a certain prayer or even to believe in him. Instead, Jesus told him "Do this and you will live." (Luke 10:28) The lawyer knew the correct answer: love God with all your heart and love your neighbor as yourself. His problem was in actually *doing it*. If he really loved God with all his heart, he would have had an open mind toward Jesus. He would have become a disciple to receive more of the teaching that empowered his life. Loving others would not become an opportunity for trying to justify himself by attempting to find out who could safely be excluded from his love. He would see what Jesus said involves a change of heart about how we view religion and its requirements. Jesus' way is not a set of rules, but a path of love toward God and Man.

Questions:

1. Why is the Law important?

2. What did the Law teach about God?

3. Does the summary Jesus gives of the most important commandments agree with God's comments about the Law in the Old Testament? Hint: check out Hosea 6:6 and Micah 6:8; 7:18.

4. Why would Jesus tell the lawyer "Do this and you will live?" How does this command apply to disciples of Jesus?

> *"But you, do not be called 'Rabbi'; for one is your Teacher, the Christ, and you are all brethren. Do not call anyone on earth your father; for One is your Father, He who is in heaven."*
>
> —Matthew 23:8-9

> *"Take heed that no one deceives you. For many will come in my name, saying, 'I am the Christ,' and will deceive many."*
>
> —Matthew 24:4-5

> *"If anyone says to you, 'Look, here is the Christ!' or 'There!' do not believe it.... Therefore if they say to you, 'Look, He is in the desert!' do not go out; or 'Look, He is in the inner rooms!' do not believe it."*
>
> —Matthew 24:23, 26

> *"Take heed that you not be deceived. For many will come in my name, saying, 'I am He', and 'The time has drawn near.' Therefore do not go after them. But when you hear of wars and commotions, do not be terrified; for these things must come to pass first, but the end will not come immediately."*
>
> —Luke 21:8-9

There is a temptation in religious community for leaders to begin to exalt themselves and Jesus makes us aware of this problem. It begins with simple titles of respect, even acknowledgement of loving roles performed by the leaders in the life of the congregation. They are teachers, so what is the harm in calling them "Teacher?" At times, they are like spiritual fathers to us, guiding and directing us through life's confusing pathways. What could be the harm in acknowledging this role and calling them "Father?"

The problem is two-fold. First, it misdirects our awareness of who is actually teaching and fathering us through them. God is the one who is active in their ministry to us, He is the one who is caring for us this way. Secondly, it is a source of great temptation to the person we address with such titles. It tempts them to think more of themselves than they ought. It will not always cause a leader to stumble at this point, but we must be careful not to be the source of anything which causes a brother to stumble. "Do not cause anyone to stumble, whether Jews, Greeks, or the church of God" (1 Corinthians 10:31) Forgetting our brotherly relationship with them, we subtly move our relationship into the area of Student/Master or Son/Father.

In the early church at Antioch, this relationship was understood. When Ananias came to Saul, he addressed him as "Brother Saul." Though Saul was not a leader in the church at the time, it reveals the mind of a disciple like Ananias, who was sensitive to the Holy Spirit and eager to do His will. His way of thinking about other believers was to consider them brothers. Peter, however, was a leader in the church from the beginning. Curiously, Jesus instructed him to think of the other disciples as his brothers rather than as "spiritual sons" or students. "Simon, Simon, Satan has asked to sift you as wheat. But I have prayed for you, Simon, that your faith may not fail. And when you have turned back, strengthen your brothers." (Luke 22:31) Many other examples may be found in the Scriptures which show God's people viewing each other as brothers and sisters.

When we look at it this way, Jesus' command for us to not call anyone "Teacher" or "Father" makes real sense. If anyone would still like to argue the point, however, is it not enough Jesus commanded it not be done? Do we need reasons for everything or can we not see he commands us for our own benefit? Let us dispense with all titles, then, between brothers and sisters in the church. They give a certain feeling of social structure and certainty, but have no value in the purposes of God for the church. In fact, they are a hindrance to accomplishing God's goals for our relationships.

Earlier, I said the first reason not to use titles was because it misdirects our attention away from God as our Teacher and Father. The other commands listed above address this issue. When leaders begin to take the attention which rightly belongs to God in the church, they begin to become puffed up with their own importance. It may not be as obvious as declaring they are the Messiah, but they may begin to feel like they are the only one who can help people. They may begin to feel *their* teaching, *their* leadership is so essential to the church, its very survival depends on *them*. The extreme case of this is found in cultic groups with strong charismatic leaders. Cults like the Branch Davidians and the one centered on Jim Jones begin with a hunger for God and end up centered on a man who believes he is Messiah.

Jesus commands his disciples to "take heed," or beware these people do not deceive them. He tells us not to believe them when they say the Messiah is "here" or "there." He tells us "do not go out" when they tell you the location of the perfect leader or Messianic group. Further, Jesus instructs us not to be deceived by this falsehood and "not to go after them."

It seems almost ridiculous people will believe someone who claims to be the Messiah when Jesus already came, accomplished his mission, and promised he would return for everyone to clearly see. How could people be deceived into thinking a church leader is the Messiah?

Usually, such a large change in thinking is not accomplished in one giant leap. It begins with small things like calling someone "Teacher" or "Father." Perhaps the title begins as "Most Reverend." Then the thinking begins to change. It becomes centered on the personality of the man rather than the Spirit of God. It may progress slowly, but the result is the same: attention is taken away from God and directed toward a person. The person may represent a movement, an idea, a theology, but they become an icon of something larger. Then their image is used to represent the idea, movement, or theology. For example, Mao Tse-tung did not proclaim he was God. The people of China, however, began to adore him as such because he represented a movement, an ideology, a final hope for a better China. As such, Mao supplanted the true Messianic hope for the people of China. All attention was focused on Mao and his Communist Party. People marched in the streets carrying pictures of Mao because they loved what he represented. They formed churches faithful to Mao and intolerant of the Gospel. They did not do this aware of the fact they were creating a Messiah, but the effect was the same. In fact, the rivalry was so strong, soon they began to persecute disciples of Jesus because he competed for the hearts and minds of the Chinese people.

China is an example of an entire nation falling under the sway of a false Christ. Any size group is vulnerable, from home-based fellowships to entire denominations. It does not matter if people are Christians or not. Jesus issued this warning to his disciples. This means even his disciples are vulnerable to the deceptive power of false Messiahs if they do not heed Jesus' warnings. A proper view of leaders in the church as brothers and sisters rather than titled Teachers and Fathers goes a long way toward inoculating us from this dangerous disease. Simple obedience to Jesus' command to beware is sufficient to protect anyone who does not understand the danger. You do not have to be a theologian to work this out, just a faithful disciple.

Questions:

1. Why are even simple titles like Teacher and Father forbidden by Jesus for religious leaders in the church?

2. How is it unfair to our leaders to use these titles?

3. Does Jesus say it may happen that people will come in his name and attempt to deceive his disciples or does he say it will happen? How does this change your attitude about the problem?

4. Why would anyone be offended if you ceased using the titles Jesus forbids?

5. Why are leaders such powerful icons for the people they lead?

"And you will hear of wars and rumors of wars. See that you are not troubled; for all these things must come to pass, but the end is not yet."

—Matthew 24:6

Jesus gave his disciples some information about the fulfillment of history, the endgame of God's plan. They asked him specifically, "when will this happen and what will be the sign of the end of the age?" (Matthew 24:3) First, Jesus answered with his warnings about false Christs. His first priority was not the amazing information about the future. Instead, he wanted to keep his disciples, including all future generations of disciples, safe in their faith. He did not want them to be deceived. This shows his priorities regarding prophecy: people first, knowledge second. Applying this priority to prophecy is a sure way to keep from getting off the track Jesus wants us to travel. He is going somewhere with us; his ultimate destination is God the Father and he wants us there with him. Knowledge about the future is a very dangerous proposition. It can influence your decisions and make you operate out of fear rather than faith. Jesus wanted his disciples to live in faith first before he gave them knowledge about the future.

He told them they "will hear of wars and rumors of wars." This is scary stuff, even for us today, perhaps especially for us today in our world of terrorism and nuclear weapons. As we saw on 11 September 2001, the course of a nation can be changed in one act of massive violence. This is not Jesus' focus, however. His main concern is his disciples. "See that you are not troubled," is his command to us, "for all these things must come to pass, but the end is not yet." Those orgies of violence called wars are not the end of the age. They are not the endgame of God's plan for history. Incredibly, Jesus' command for his disciples is for them not to be troubled by all this violence.

Not to be troubled? This is amazing! Wars impact not only individuals, but entire *generations*. It is thought World War I brought down the British Empire because an entire generation of youth no longer believed in the concept of the British Empire after betrayal by their leaders on the battlefields of Europe. World War I is thought to be the cause of cynicism among almost the entire generation of young people who passed into adulthood at that time, not only in England, but also around the world.

Still, Jesus instructs us not to be troubled by this situation. It is not the end of the world. God will have the last word, not Man and his violence. God has a plan for history, it is not a random set of events at the mercy of ignorant or evil men. Jesus imparted to us more than information *about* the end of the world, he gave us an attitude with which to face it. There is no more difficult fact to face than death. Every individual experiences at least discomfort when considering their own demise. It can cause great angst when you begin to think about the end of a civilization. The world as it has been known, the order men have worked so hard to construct, is all thrown into chaos. It is even more difficult to consider the end of history, extinction of the human race. Scientists tell us some time in the future, the Sun will run out of nuclear fuel and ultimately burn out. If and when that happens, everything on Earth will be destroyed. All of history, every accomplishment, piece of art, every great idea formed in the mind of Man will be extinguished along with all the beauty of nature. Feeling depressed yet?

The point is Jesus is not overly concerned about these things. He is more concerned about *you*. If the Sun burned out tomorrow, it will not be the end of *you*, because God has a plan for you that involves being with Him. All of Jesus' focus and attention is on this fact, all of his effort in ministry. He even went to the Cross for this purpose, to make a way for you, his disciple, to be with God. A disciple of Jesus is not to chase after theories of the end time. Instead, he is to be secure in the knowledge of God's plan and communicate the plan faithfully to others so they can also become disciples of Jesus.

Questions:

1. What was Jesus' immediate answer to his disciples when they asked him about the end of the world?

2. What is God's aim at the end of history?

3. Why are wars so troubling?

4. Why would Jesus seem so untroubled by wars and news of war?

"Learn this parable from the fig tree: when its branch has already become tender and puts forth leaves, you know that summer is near. So you also, when you see all these things, know that it is near—at the doors!"
—Matthew 24:32-33

"Now when these things begin to happen, look up and lift your heads, because your redemption draws near."
—Luke 21:28

"Watch therefore, for you do not know what hour your Lord is coming.... Therefore you also be ready, for the Son of Man is coming at an hour you do not expect."
—Matthew 24:42, 44

"Let your waist be girded and your lamps burning; and you yourselves be like men who wait for their master, when he will return from the wedding, that when he comes and knocks they may open to him immediately.... Therefore, you also be ready, for the Son of Man is coming at an hour you do not expect."
—Luke 12:35-36,40

"Take heed to yourselves, lest your hearts be weighed down with carousing, drunkenness, and cares of this life, and that Day come on you unexpectedly. For it will come as a snare on all those who dwell on the face of the whole earth. Watch therefore, and pray always that you may be counted worthy to escape all these things that will come to pass, and to stand before the Son of Man."
—Luke 21: 34-36

Jesus has a very curious way of responding to his disciples' question about the end of the age. He gives them some very sketchy details to look for and then he tells them to learn a lesson from a tree. By looking at a fig tree you can tell when it is about to bloom. In the same way, he says, his disciples should watch for the events he described and know the time is near, "at the doors!" he says. His answer to their question was to tell them to be aware and read the signs around them. Then he goes on to give further instructions.

These instructions have nothing to do with how to respond to the end of the age. The first tells us to "lift up your heads, for your redemption is near." In effect, Jesus says, when you see everything I described happening, look up to God because He is about to redeem you from the problems you see. So the focus of a disciple of Jesus is not to be on the problems in the world. It is to be on God, knowing whatever the problems are, God has something good in store for his disciples. Look up and expect what is coming – it is going to be good!

Jesus also instructs us to watch and be ready for his return. He does not want his disciples falling asleep at the wheel, or worse, forgetting their master's commands and living like the world around them. To reinforce this, he told a story about virgins who were holding lamps for a bridegroom's arrival to the wedding feast. He was delayed, so some of them had to go get more oil for their lamps. When the bridegroom came, the ones who went to the market were left out of the feast; the doors were already locked. Jesus wants us to "Let your waist be girded and your lamps burning." Be ready for his return, busy doing what he commanded to be done. Even with the detailed signs he described, Jesus said, "the Son of Man is coming at an hour you do not expect."

He specifically commanded us to "take heed to yourselves" so we do not become weighed down with partying and the cares of this life. The end of the age will come like a snare on everyone living aboard Planet Earth. A snare was a trap used to catch animals. One type would be tied to a tree limb. As the animal moved through the forest and stepped on the snare, it would spring the trap and be caught unaware by the entangling rope or net. Even a large beast like a lion or bear was helpless when the trappers came to claim them. Jesus told his disciples his coming would be like the springing of such a trap. Because of this, he commanded them to watch and pray so they could escape the terrible things which are going to happen and to "stand before the Son of Man."

Each disciple knows he will ultimately stand before God and give account for his life. What Jesus said, however, is you will be caught by surprise, like an animal in a trap, by that time. Would you not want Jesus to find you busy doing as he commanded when the trap springs? Then you need have no shame being caught in the action. But it is possible for disciples to leave off doing the will of Jesus and instead worry about the things the world does: making a good living, furthering your career, enjoying parties with your friends. He warned us in advance; do not turn aside to these things. He wants us to be watchful, prayerful, fully aware the time is short.

Even if Jesus does not return in your lifetime to the earth, your personal death could occur instantaneously. You may not have time to do anything about it. Once, I had a friend killed in a motorcycle accident. He loved riding his Harley Davidson with his wife behind him. One weekend, they were cruising on some country roads and a car came over the middle of the road and struck them head on. My friend's wife survived the accident and told me the only thing he had time to say was, "Hang on!"

It can happen that quickly. Or, we may live to an old age and Jesus returns to earth in our lifetime. Either way, he told us we will stand before him. Our lamps should be burning brightly to welcome his return.

Questions:

1. Where should the focus of a disciple be when the problems in the world become so intense?

2. Even if you recognized all the signs of the end of the age, does Jesus say it will arrive when you expect it?

3. What should be the posture of a disciple of Jesus during the period of waiting for Jesus' return to earth?

4. Does knowing the end time matter? Why or why not?

"Take, eat; this is My body....Drink from it, all of you. For this is My blood of the new covenant, which is shed for many for the remission of sins."
—Matthew 26:26-28

"This is My body which is given for you; do this in remembrance of Me."
—Luke 22:19

At the Last Supper, the night of his arrest, Jesus told his disciples to eat bread and drink wine. He explained to them the bread was his body broken for them and the drink was his blood, shed for the forgiveness of sins. This explanation forever puts to rest any question what was Jesus' purpose on earth. He was at the final hour, the moment before the accomplishment of the great purpose God had for him before he was even born. This was the perfect moment to explain his mission and he did it using elements with great religious significance: bread and wine.

While understanding the complete significance of the Last Supper is way beyond the scope of this book, it is relevant to examine his commands at this meal. He told them to "Take, eat" and "Drink from it, all of you." Disciples of Jesus are told to take the bread and wine, eat and drink them. Re-enacting this ceremony in Communion, disciples of Jesus are obeying his command. The command is not for some only, but for all disciples. All are to "Take, eat" and "Drink."

Future generations of disciples are included in this command also because Jesus said, "do this in remembrance of Me." We are commanded to remember Jesus in re-enacting this Last Supper. Jesus did not give reasons for this, he simply ordered it to be done. There are, however, some interesting benefits for disciples who obey.

First, we are transported back through time to the historic event of the Last Supper. We were not there with Peter, James, John, Judas, and the others. By taking Communion, however, we in some way participate in the same event. The event itself was timeless, the fulfillment of God's mission to the world for the forgiveness of sins. It is as if Jesus were saying, "Now, I've spent a lot of time with you, teaching you many things. I've given you many commands and instructed you about the Kingdom of God. This is the climax of my story, this is what it is all about. God is going to forgive all sins because of what is about to happen tomorrow. Keep this ceremonial meal as a reminder to everyone about me and what I have accomplished."

It is easy to ignore preaching and teaching about the Bible. Heads nod in church, eyes glaze over, and suddenly you find yourself thinking about Sunday afternoon football or how to keep the kids quiet in public. Then comes Communion. It actually requires you to do something besides listening. You have to take the bread and eat it. You have to drink the wine. It makes you stop and think about why you are doing these things. Then you remember Jesus. This is what he wanted all along. It is wonderful to hear good preaching in church, sing good songs, and fellowship with other disciples. But for the disciple of Jesus, he is the center of the whole story. He is the main event. What he accomplished on the cross is worth remembering over and over so we never forget. It is worth doing publicly in front of a gathered community and shared together. It is this important.

Quite simply, without the blood of Jesus, there is no new covenant, no new agreement between God and Man. We would be stuck under the old agreement, the one promising the curse of death as a punishment for our sin. We may not completely understand Communion, but it is not an optional part of our Christian faith. It is a command Jesus gave to his disciples for all time, or at least until we can share a meal with him face to face. Obeying this command can help a disciple keep focused on Jesus and avoid being distracted by the concerns of the world. Communion was so important to Mother Teresa, she would meditate about its meaning every night. For her, it was an irreplaceable source of strength. Going without Communion for her would be like asking an engine to run without fuel. It could not happen.

If, somehow, Jesus really is present as he said in the bread and wine and we really do share fellowship with him by eating and drinking, then it is easy to see why Mother Teresa was correct. A disciple can do nothing without his master. Or, as Jesus said elsewhere, "apart from me you can do nothing." (John 15:5)

Questions:

1. Do Jesus' commands at the Last Supper apply to disciples today as well as those present at the historic event? Who did he order to eat and drink the meal?

2. What are some benefits of obeying the command to eat and drink Communion?

3. How does Communion focus attention on the Gospel?

4. Why would Communion be essential for a disciple of Jesus?

"Watch and pray lest you enter into temptation. The spirit indeed is willing, but the flesh is weak."
—Matthew 26:41

"Pray that you may not enter temptation."
—Luke 22:40

This specific order was issued to Peter, James, and John in the Garden of Gethsemane. Jesus had earlier ordered them to come with him apart and "watch" with him. The sense of the Greek word is to "stay awake" with him. When he returned to their position, Jesus found them all asleep. Then he issued the order above with an explanation. Because of the explanation, this command applies not only to Peter, James, and John, but also to all disciples of Jesus.

He told us something very valuable: "Stay awake and pray so you do not enter into temptation." How easily we can drift off asleep at the helm of our lives! How boring life can be at times and so our attention fades until we are almost fully unaware of what is happening to us. All this watching and praying Jesus wants us to do is to keep us from falling into temptation. It seems the devil and our own sinful cravings are simply waiting for our spiritual man to lose interest in life. Then they can move in and flash interesting and soothing alternatives to following Jesus.

The alternatives may be seemingly harmless like really falling asleep as Peter did. The point is the alternative keeps us from living out the will of God. Peter had no idea by falling asleep he would be completely unprepared for the treason of Judas. If he had been awake, perhaps he would have understood what was happening had been predicted by Jesus and it had to occur. Maybe he would not have pulled out his sword and cut off the ear of the High Priest's servant. Or maybe he would not have denied Jesus. Who knows? What we do know is Jesus commanded them to keep watch and pray so they would not give in to the temptations they would face.

We also face temptations as we follow Jesus. Every day, they await our inattention to his word as the opening for testing us. Are we aware of them? Do we know what they are when they occur? A wide-awake person deals with these temptations much better than someone distracted and lulled into a false sense of security, someone who is, in effect, sleeping.

A helmsman for a ship stands a "watch" at the helm. During that time, he is expected to remain not only awake, but also alert. The safety of the whole ship depends on him steering the course he was ordered to maintain. Even slight errors can grow into enormous differences in distance over time. A one-degree difference in course translates into an error of 35 yards every mile. This may not seem like much, but a ten-day voyage with this kind of error would place the ship 42 miles from its intended position. You could miss an island this way and be lost at sea! All of this can be avoided by "watching."

In the same way, Jesus wants us to maintain the course God has plotted out for our lives. If we begin to stray from the course, it is relatively simple to get back on track once we discover the error. But if we are not watching, soon we are far off course and very far from the place God intends. Temptation is like this, as it distracts us just enough so we "fall asleep" spiritually and become unaware of our course error. By the time we awaken to what has happened, it can be too late to change course without causing major pain to ourselves and others. We have drifted so far that getting back on track requires a drastic shift and extra effort simply to get where Jesus intended for us to be all along if only we had been paying attention.

The second component of Jesus' command is to pray. It is not enough to simply watch or stay awake. We must ask God to give us wisdom, strength, and courage to withstand the temptations we know will come. Jesus himself prayed in Gethsemane for God's will to be done in his life. He did not want to go to the cross. He even asked his Father to "let this cup pass from me." Jesus realized, however, in his prayer, what he wanted more than anything was to accomplish his Father's will. "Nevertheless, not as I will, but as you will." (Matthew 26:39) I believe Jesus received the strength he needed for his ultimate test in this hour of prayer in Gethsemane. He was trying to pass on this wisdom to his disciples when he told them to watch and pray. He wanted us to know we need to be awake and we need our Father's help in prayer if we are going to make it through life's trials.

His statement after the command is simply a fact: "The spirit is willing, but the flesh is weak." We may *want* to follow God with all our heart, but we will find ourselves tripped up by our own weaknesses. Wanting to do God's will is not enough to bring us through temptation unscathed. We need divine help and this help is available to us in prayer. Peter, James, and John failed that night, even as we so often fail in this matter of staying awake and praying. A bad situation was worse than it had to be for them because of this failure. How many of our bad situations are made worse because we also have failed to "watch and pray?"

Questions:

1. What is the purpose of watching and praying?

2. What does it mean for us to "watch?"

3. How can a small inattention to detail translate into large mistakes in life?

4. Why is watching or being awake not enough to see us through temptation unharmed?

5. If we do find ourselves in trouble because of our lack of attention and prayer, is our situation unrecoverable? Can we still get back on course with God? What may we still have to deal with, however?

"Put your sword in its place, for all who take the sword will perish by the sword."

—Matthew 26:52

"Put your sword into the sheathe. Shall I not drink the cup my Father has given me?"

—John 18:11

Jesus gave Peter a clear command regarding his use of violence in an attempt to defend his master. He tells him to put the sword back in its sheathe. The following statement explains the reason for this instruction. Jesus tells Peter, "all who take the sword will perish by the sword." This is a certainty coming from the mouth of Jesus. It is not, "you may get hurt that way, Peter." Dying a violent death is assured for everyone who uses violence as their method of resolving conflict.

It is difficult to think of a more just cause than defending Jesus. Even in his own case, however, Jesus did not want Peter using a sword to defend him. He had other ideas about what was happening. Jesus knew it was his Father's will for him to be betrayed and die on the cross; it was "the cup my Father has given me." To violently oppose what was happening would be to oppose what God was doing.

There may be cases where violence is needed to defend innocent life, even your own life. It is probably not the will of God for people to die as murder victims. It is important, however, for disciples of Jesus to weigh very carefully the decision to use violence. Are we certain we are not simply giving in to the temptation of taking up the sword? Anger and bitterness can easily cause us to lose our better judgment. We could find ourselves harming or killing another human being for no other reason than because we avoided a more difficult approach. Perhaps, if we are in the military, we could find ourselves killing someone for no other reason than because someone told us to kill.

When I was a young submarine officer, my ship was designated as one that would carry nuclear weapons. Immediately upon reporting for duty aboard the ship, the Weapons Officer called me into his stateroom and had me sign some paperwork. He was required to ask me one question: "If you are ordered to launch nuclear weapons, will you do so?" Of course, the expected answer was "yes." Any other answer would have seen me escorted off the ship and assigned to some other duty station. No submarine could afford to carry an officer that had qualms about following orders to launch a nuclear missile.

What I realized later, as I began to walk closer with God, was by launching a nuclear weapon, I could kill thousands of innocent people without even knowing it. You do not aim a nuclear missile when it is launched; the computer controls it. You do not know who is being bombed. It may seem the person who launched the missile bears no responsibility for the deaths of those thousands because he would simply be following orders. As I began to meditate upon the words of Jesus and think about his statement to Peter, I realized launching a nuclear weapon against an unknown target is not something I want to have on my conscience.

The key to understanding this command of Jesus is his understanding of God's will. Jesus clearly knew what God wanted him to do. It was difficult to accept, even for him, but he knew his mission. Opposing the betrayal and arrest would only detract from accomplishing God's plan. Therefore, Jesus told Peter to put his sword away. We cannot forget, however, the statement he made to Peter as if quoting a physical law: "all who take the sword will perish by the sword." It instructs us even now, we disciples who do not stand in Gethsemane with him as Judas approached. Instead, we have enemies who mistreat us, ungodly governments who oppose us, and people who sin against us in a multitude of ways. Too often, we have assumed violence is the only way to deal with our problems. It is a "default" solution. When all else fails, we know we can at least shoot our opponents dead and the problem will be resolved.

In a world where violence seems to be the ultimate trump card, Jesus tells us we should put away our swords so we do not die by the sword. Jesus does not want us to die violent deaths. He does not want us sucked into thinking only weaponry can solve problems and keep us safe. Gangs in inner-city neighborhoods are a good example of what Jesus is trying to help us avoid. The neighborhoods they live in are rough. Gangs teach their members in order to survive in this violent world, they must be the most violent, the strongest survivors. Sadly, these gangsters live short, miserable lives, unaware there even is another way to live.

Questions:

1. What is the key to understanding why Jesus prohibited Peter from using his sword in Jesus' defense?

2. What does this command tell you Jesus does not want to happen to his disciples?

3. What situations have you been placed in that tempt you to use violence against others?

4. Why does violence seem to be a "trump card?"

> "Go therefore and make disciples of all nations, baptizing them in the name of the Father and of the Son and of the Holy Spirit, teaching them to observe all things I have commanded you; and lo, I am with you always, even to the end of the age."
>
> —Matthew 28:19-20

Here is the famous command called the Great Commission. In it, Jesus is telling his disciples to go out and make disciples from all nations of people. He tells them this as a result of revealing "All authority has been given to me in heaven and on earth." (Matthew 28:18) Because Jesus has been given all authority by his Father God, he wants his disciples to make people of all nations into disciples as well. The extent of his authority extends far beyond the Jewish nation.

This alone was a radical idea to the Jews. Notice how much trouble it caused in the early history of the Church: Peter is told to share the Good News of Jesus with Gentiles (Acts 10), baptizes them, and is opposed when he returns to Jerusalem by Jewish believers (Acts 11:1-18). God had always shown grace, but the Jewish people thought his grace was reserved for them as his chosen people. The Great Commission smashes this misconception with a direct command. Not only are disciples of Jesus to welcome people from all nations to come to faith in Jesus, they are expected to *go* and find the Gentiles and make disciples of them. This involves crossing cultural boundaries at least and often geographic ones as well.

It is impossible to take this command seriously without thinking of the people who are not disciples; whole nations of people without anyone following Jesus. Spreading the good news about Jesus is the first priority Jesus himself had for his disciples when he revealed his universal divine authority to them. This good news was not simply a proclamation of headlines: "Jesus died for your sins, repent and live!" Instead, Jesus commanded *disciples be made.* The first step in making a disciple is belief and baptism for the forgiveness of sins. This much, John the Baptist did as well. What Jesus added was the order to *teach* the new disciples *"all things I have commanded you."*

This means every new follower of Jesus must be taught every command of Jesus. It is the reason I decided to write this book. Many people become believers in Jesus but do not know enough to even begin to follow him as a disciple. They are not even aware Jesus has expectations of his disciples. These commands are what separate *believers* from *disciples.* Jesus is not looking for admiring fans like a sports team. He is looking for you to join the team yourself, begin to practice the plays, become proficient enough to be a champion yourself rather than watch him do it and cheer. Jesus is looking for commitment. Knowing and obeying his commands demonstrates our commitment to Jesus.

Now many people will rightly point out it is impossible for a Christian to follow all the commands of Jesus all the time; they are too stringent, against our human nature, beyond our grasp. They certainly are all of these things. A fair examination of these commands quickly shows Jesus demands far more of us than we are capable of delivering, which is why the next part of the Great Commission verse is so important:

"and lo, I am with you always, even to the end of the age."

Jesus told his disciples this world-wide movement of discipleship is far beyond anything any single human or even a generation of humans can accomplish. None of those hearing his words that day lived to see "the end of the age." Even now, we have not seen its end. The new age began when Jesus came on the earth, taught, died, and was raised up to heaven. That new age has not yet ended. We continue to live under the shadow of his Great Commission, making disciples of all nations until he himself returns in all his glory to rule them personally. We do not, however, do this alone; Jesus himself promised to be *with* us until the end of the age.

The work of discipleship continues in our hearts personally and out in the world through our teaching of the commands of Jesus, his Standing Orders. On my Navy ship, by teaching the Standing Orders to newer junior officers, every officer became more acquainted with them. The same is true of our own discipleship. By teaching others the commands of Jesus, we ourselves grow to love and appreciate them more. They become "written on our hearts" (Jeremiah 31:33). When God's Law is written on your heart, it becomes the desire of your heart. As the desires of a disciple of Jesus change, so change his actions. A person will do what he most desires.

Buddhism teaches desire must be eliminated in order to achieve enlightenment. Jesus teaches he will replace your selfish, sinful desires with his own righteous ones. The process of discipleship is nothing more nor less than learning and appropriating the desires of Jesus for yourself. It does not stop there, however, because the last desire we see in the life of Jesus is in this very command from Matthew 28. His desire is all nations of people become his followers and have God's Law written on their hearts. This takes the individual disciple of Jesus full-circle: you begin by learning to follow Jesus yourself, but you end up having the desire to see others following him also; people you have never met. Thus, discipleship is both the beginning and end of every believer; the last and great command of Jesus.

Questions:

1. Who does Jesus want to be his disciples?

2. Why does Jesus want them to be his disciples?

3. How is discipleship not simply "the proclamation of headlines"?

4. How would you answer the objection it is impossible to follow the commands of Jesus as a disciple?

5. How does Jesus view desire differently than Buddha? What difference does this make for his disciples?

"From that time on, Jesus began to preach, 'Repent, for the kingdom of heaven is near.'"
—Matthew 4:17

"The time is fulfilled, and the kingdom of God is at hand. Repent, and believe in the gospel."
—Mark 1:15

This is the earliest recorded statement of Jesus' preaching. It contained a simple message: repent and believe. The first part of this command is the same as John the Baptist's preaching. He announced in the Judean wilderness: "Repent, for the kingdom of heaven is near." (Matthew 3:2) Great crowds came out to hear John preach this message. Many of the tax collectors and "sinners", those who had shown no regard for God before, began turning to God after hearing John.

John, however, ended his message with this: "I baptize you with water for repentance. But after me will come one who is more powerful than I, whose sandals I am not fit to carry. He will baptize you with the Holy Spirit and with fire." (Matthew 3:11) This prophet preached all people needed to turn to God and be washed with water as a sign of their new beginning, leaving their old sinful ways behind. He preached this not in Jerusalem, not in the temple, nor in synagogues, but out in the Judean wilderness by the Jordan River. It was as if John were making the statement this message was directly from God, no ruling elite controlled it, it came for all people, including the elite. No one owned the wilderness and no one except God owned John the Baptizer. Yet even John declared the Messiah would follow him and was more powerful. It was Messiah's kingdom John preached about; it was His people John wanted to make ready to hear their King.

When the King began his public ministry, it was fitting his message began with John's: repent. Jesus took it a step farther, however. He said the kingdom is "near", "the time is fulfilled", and "the kingdom of God is at hand." What he is announcing is John's prophecy and preparation is coming true in Jesus' life and preaching. What Jesus had to deliver was "good news" he wanted everyone to believe. With this good news is the Holy Spirit John spoke about, the baptism with fire to which a dunking in the Jordan River was only a prelude. Repentance was the preparation to receive something much better: the Lord himself.

The command to repent is timeless. It is a command to turn away from our disregard of God and our regard for ourselves or the world. He commands us to turn towards God and get ready to receive something incredible, something absolutely amazing! A good water bath gets you washed off fairly well, but you'll soon get dirty again. Getting doused with fire is another thing altogether. You will be marked forever; your body will never be the same again. So it is with the difference between John's baptism and Jesus'.

It is possible to go through life continually repenting of sin and wanting to change, but not actually accomplishing it. What Jesus offered was a completely different way of living; a new life, born in the Holy Spirit. It is life in the kingdom of God Jesus spoke about, not a new religion. All the rest of Jesus' preaching was an outline for his disciples what this kingdom looked like, how its citizens behaved, and its driving force. Every command of Jesus gives us insight into what his kingdom will be for eternity, but also how we are to enact it on earth in the meantime.

Another aspect of this command to notice is "the kingdom of heaven is near" and "the time is fulfilled, the kingdom of God is at hand." There is an immediacy to Jesus' command to repent. The kingdom we have been waiting for over the ages has come in the person and ministry of Jesus. He fulfilled every prophecy of the kingdom. He taught what kind of people are its citizens. No more waiting. If you keep waiting after this, you are going to miss what God is doing; it's here in everything Jesus lived and said. There are no more great prophets after Jesus revealing the Word of the Lord. Instead, the Word of the Lord revealed himself and opened up with an invitation for all to come and believe the incredibly good news. May none of us be found with an unbelieving attitude toward him.

Questions:

1. How is the early preaching of Jesus tied to John the Baptist and his preaching?

2. What was different about Jesus' preaching?

3. How is the concept of "the kingdom of God" important for understanding the preaching and commands of Jesus?

4. How is a citizen of God's kingdom "doused with fire"? What implications does this have for daily life?

5. Why did Jesus preach repentance with a sense of immediacy?

"Follow me."

—Mark 2:14

This is one of the shortest and simplest commands Jesus gave, yet it is probably the most important. The same immediacy is present in this command as in his previous admonishment to repent and believe the good news. There is a sense that after delivering the command, Jesus is waiting for you to respond. Levi the tax collector, to whom Jesus issued this command, certainly felt this immediacy. He was sitting there at his tax booth with money piled up in front of him, doing his job. Imagine tablets and writing utentils on a desk which he used to mark down who paid their taxes. Think of people lined up to see the tax collector, each carrying their alloted payment to the Roman government. There were probably soldiers standing behind him to enforce the law and ensure no one interefered with the payment of taxes. No government survives very long without making sure it can collect taxes. What Levi was doing was serious business.

Up walks Jesus and tells him, "Follow me." Then he is standing there, waiting. How will Levi respond?

Mark tells us simply, "Levi got up and followed him." When faced with the choice between a new life of following Jesus as a disciple and remaining in the lucrative business of collecting Roman taxes, Levi did not hesitate. He just walked away.

Think about the people standing in line, his assistants behind the desk, the soldiers guarding the cash. What were they thinking? They must have been amazed to see this man simply get up and walk away after Jesus.

It is really no different today for any potential disciple of Jesus. He will walk up into your life, in the very *midst* of your life, papers strewn all over your desk or dirty dishes piled up in the sink and tell you to follow him. He offers no apparent solutions to your problems, does not tell you everything is going to work out fine, gives no insurance and no guarantees. Jesus simply offers an invitation, then waits to see how you respond.

We often think we need answers before we can follow Jesus. Somehow we think he needs to satisfy our reasoning or sense of security. He is under no obligation to do either. The invitation is there, simply to follow him. We do not even know where he is going most of the time. This command is an offer to trust. Jesus offers the highest honor one can possibly have in this world: to be a disciple of the King. Our acceptance or denial of this offer depends completely upon whether we trust him or not. And like it or not, Jesus did not wait all day at Levi's desk. There comes a time when he will move on and the chance to follow has passed. That is why the immediacy of this command is so important. It also explains the importance of a prepared heart, one which has repented of sin and turned toward God. For the repentant heart does not need to think about this offer; it is ready to get up and go. Levi helps us understand the purpose of John the Baptist. As John quoted from Isaiah 40:3, "Prepare the way for the Lord, make straight paths for him." By hearing this preaching and obeying, Levi was ready to respond to Jesus when he stood there in the noonday sun and told him to follow.

Questions:

1. How does the story of Levi show the immediacy of Jesus' command to follow him? What was Levi's other name and how is this significant? (Hint: see Matthew 9:9)

2. Levi had important things going on in his life at the time Jesus appeared to him. What important things are happening in your life which could prevent you from answering his command to follow him?

3. What does it mean that Jesus "gives no insurance and no guarantees"? What does Jesus promise for his disciples? (Hint: see John 16:33, John 17:14,15,19, Matthew 19:29)

4. How does the story of Levi show the importance of John the Baptist and his message?

5. Are there people in your life standing around like those soldiers and people in line for Levi who are amazed you "got up from your desk" to follow Jesus?

"He who has ears to hear, let him hear."
—Mark 4:9

"Take heed what you hear. With the same measure you use, it will be measured to you; and to you who hear, more will be given."
—Mark 4:24

"Take heed how you hear. For whoever has, more will be given; and whoever does not have, whatever he seems to have will be taken from him."
—Luke 8:18

Jesus commands us to listen to what we hear of his teaching. His concept of "listen" extends beyond the mere hearing of words into practicing a way of life. Essentially, Jesus told his disciples to fashion their lives around his teaching. For those who had "ears to hear, let him hear." Often, we hear words and even intellectually assent they are true, but we do not allow the words to form our thinking. Instead, we sit in judgment over the words, deciding what we will allow into our lives and what we will keep outside. Jesus does not want it to be this way with his words to us. He wants us to make our minds actually hear every word he said and incorporate them into the way our minds work.

Doing this has two results. First, the amount of his teaching we allow into our minds is the measure of benefit we will get out of what we hear. God will measure out exactly as much as you allow in. Once a disciple takes in his Word and incorporates it into life, that disciple is ready for more Word to be measured out, to receive another portion. "And to you who hear, more will be given." So if we want to receive more from God, we must first make use of what we have already received. Do not expect more from God than you have already digested. He will not fill you with more until you have used up what you have been given. He does not want his disciples walking around spiritually constipated!

Secondly, absorption of God's Word and perseverance in acting it out will result in producing good fruit in your life. This good fruit is the reward of patiently watering the seed of God's Word and waiting for it to produce. This good fruit is the "candy" everyone wants: peace, self-control, enjoyment of life. All people want to live happy lives. Still, these fruits only come to those who are willing to receive Jesus' words and patiently wait for them to grow. Immediately preceding the Luke 8:18 citation of this command is the Parable of the Sower. In this story, Jesus tells about a farmer who sowed seed in various places. The seed is the Word of God. Only those who hear the word with "a noble and good heart", "retain it, and by persevering produce a crop" are the ones who see any benefit from receiving the seed. On every other soil, on all the other people, the seed of the word is wasted.

The last implication of this command is whoever does not truly "hear" the word of God will lose even what little bit he thinks he possesses. Or, as Jesus says, "whatever he seems to have will be taken from him." So even if someone appears to be a good person, to have a noble heart, to seek love and peace with all people, if this did not come from hearing and receiving the word of God, it will be taken from them. Only the word of God bears lasting and true fruit. Only our response to Jesus' teaching will determine the quality of our character and a truly happy life. No wonder Jesus admonishes us to "take heed how you hear"!

Questions:

1. What is Jesus' concept of "listening"? How is it different from hearing in the way you are used to practicing?

2. What are the results of listening the way Jesus wants?

3. What happens when someone does not "listen" the way Jesus wants?

4. How does this command change the way you view the teaching of Jesus?

5. Why do you think Jesus brought this issue of "listening" up to his disciples?

6. How can you "take heed how you hear"?

> *"Go home to your friends and tell them what great things God has done for you, and how he has had compassion on you."*
>
> —Mark 5:19

Jesus healed a demon-possessed man, casting the demons into a herd of pigs. These pigs ran madly into the lake off a cliff. The people of that region were so annoyed by this event they begged Jesus to leave their neighborhood. As Jesus was getting into the boat to leave, the formerly demon-possessed man begged to go with him, but Jesus instead gave him this command. Certainly Jesus had specific reasons for giving this command to him. Jesus was unable to stay and preach to the rest of the people, the people were unwilling to listen to his preaching after this dramatic display of power and authority, and perhaps the economic loss of the pigs angered the wealthy owner of the herd. So the demon-possessed man was the only person who could tell others in that region what had happened and give the straight story. He would make sure God received the glory and everyone would know God had sent Jesus to them to be heard by them.

Still, the command applies to every disciple of Jesus because every disciple has experienced the overwhelming power and love of God in their lives. Every disciple has become a disciple because they considered "normal life" no longer satisfying. Each disciple has followed after Jesus in a specific way, even though some are prevented from leaving their neighborhoods just like this man. And all disciples, given the chance, would beg to go with Jesus rather than be left behind; their love and desire for Him is so strong.

Who will tell our families and friends the great things of God if we will not tell them? Why would we hold back from telling them the awesome wonders of His power and the compassion we have experienced in Jesus? There are, in fact, many obstacles. First, our family and friends think they know us. After all, they knew us from the time we were young, watched us grow and develop into who we are today. So if the demon-possessed man went home, everyone would know he was the crazy guy who lived in the cemetery cutting himself. This pre-judgment can be intimidating. But this is exactly why Jesus wants us to tell them what God has done! Only God can make a crazy man sane or a homosexual straight or a drug addict totally healed. It is the sheer impossibility of the task that magnifies the glory of God in those who hear the news.

Second, it is much easier to run away to new surroundings and a different situation than it is to remain where you were in bondage. The temptation to get away and change the scenery can keep us from fulfilling what God wants to do through us in the people and places we know. God may call us away to different people and a broader world, but He does not want us to abandon the one where He found us. God is interested in all people; this is why Jesus sailed over to the other side of the lake in the first place. He wants your friends and family to hear the good news as well!

A third obstacle is embarrassment. Often we are embarrassed to share what God has done for us because we fear our friends and family will reject us. They are so dear to us we dare not risk their rejection. This is a very real concern. It places our commitment to Jesus against the strongest ties we have with this world: the people closest to us. Yet, even here, the fear can be mostly in our minds. It is a real possibility people will reject the good news of Jesus – after all, they begged him to leave the region when he healed the demon-possessed man! Still, even the hardest skeptics could not deny the man's life was much better after he met Jesus. Even though friends and family may ridicule your story of God's power and compassion, they cannot deny your life is different. Only if we allow our lives to remain the same would this be possible. But Jesus has come and changed everything and made a way for us to be free of the past, looking forward to the future, and here to tell about what God has done for us.

Despite the obstacles, telling our friends and family what God has done for us in meeting Jesus for ourselves is not only a good thing to do, it is what he *wants* us to do, what he *commands* us to do. So if we were begging to go in the boat with him, would we be willing to wait a bit and stay home awhile until we've told our story?

Questions:

1. Why does this command apply to every disciple of Jesus, not just the man from whom the demons were cast out?

2. What are the obstacles in the way of sharing what God has done for us in Christ?

3. How can each obstacle be overcome?

> *"In whatever place you enter a house, stay there until you depart from that place. And whoever will not receive you nor hear you, when you depart from there, shake off the dust under your feet as a testimony against them. Assuredly, I say to you, it will be more tolerable for Sodom and Gomorrah in the day of judgment than for that city!"*
> —Mark 6:10-11

Jesus gave specific instructions to his disciples when he sent them on mission. He told them to stay with one household in each town until they left the town. This command may seem strange. We might think it better to spread around and stay with different people, perhaps feeling guilty about overstaying a welcome. Jesus told them not to do it that way. There may be several reasons for this.

One welcoming household provided an opportunity to really establish relationships beyond the introductory phase. Once the initial glow of a visit is over, the inevitable conflicts must be faced and worked out. A deeper relationship would become possible for the visitor and the host, beyond gratitude and any feelings of obligation. A *family*-type relationship would begin to form. Mutual dependence, trust, and reliance develop. Skipping around to different houses short-circuits the developing relationship. This is exactly the kind of relatioship Jesus wanted to encourage among his disciples: mutual dependence, trust, and brotherly love. What a simple and useful way to accomplish this goal!

In addition, the hosts of this household received the benefit of not only hearing the Gospel preached, but also the living out of a Christian life in the flesh of the disciple. It served as a pattern for discipleship for them. Paul wrote, "Therefore I urge you to imitate me." (1 Corinthians 4:16) The church in Corinth knew what he meant because Paul had actually lived among them for an extended period of time. The people who hosted him would have seen how he handled every situation, how he prayed, how he worshiped God, how he dealt with conflict and disappointment. It is impossible to hide these things from the people with whom you live. So this command of Jesus also served an important purpose in discipleship for those who were hosting his disciples.

The host household also served as the seed for a house-church in a new town. Paul wrote of "the church that meets at their house." (Romans 16:5) We know Paul preached "publicly and from house to house." (Acts 20:20) The early Jerusalem church "broke bread in their homes and ate together with glad and sincere hearts" (Acts 2:46). The preaching of the Gospel was always followed by an infant church meeting in the house of a believer. Often, this household was probably the one which hosted the disciple who first preached the good news in town. By staying in one household, the disciple established a pattern of meeting that would continue with the fellowship of believers long after he left. Long before churches had buildings, they had believing households.

The first part of this command dealt with the people who received the Gospel. In the second part, Jesus told his disciples how to handle the situation when no one in town would receive their message. *"And whoever will not receive you nor hear you, when you depart from there, shake off the dust under your feet as a testimony against them."* Shaking the dust off your feet is a symbolic gesture. It basically says, "I came here, but you would not receive me. I have done my part, but you wanted no part of the Kingdom I came to share. Therefore, I will carry no part of you with me." Shaking the dust of the town off your feet shakes off the only part of those people remaining with you on your shoes. They refused to enter into true relationship with the disciple and Jesus is saying the disciple should let them know they have missed their chance of having any part in the Kingdom the disciple preached. The disciple and the message of the Kingdom is moving on now to others who will receive it. And to put it in context, Jesus says this: *"Assuredly, I say to you, it will be more tolerable for Sodom and Gomorrah in the day of judgment than for that city!"* He lets them know the refusal of the Gospel message and its messengers puts a town in worse standing with God than even the notoriously sinful cities of Sodom and Gomorrah!

This command of Jesus sets up a perspective for every disciple of Christ. It establishes the relationship-basis of the church, its initial structure, a pattern for discipleship, and even the consequences for refusal to receive the disciple and his message. This perspective can help us all stay on track with what Jesus considers important: transmission of the message of his Kingdom; the living out of the Kingdom in real people; and the truth of what refusal to enter his Kingdom means.

Questions:

1. Why would Jesus care about whether or not his disciples stayed in one house or many in their travels to spread the Gospel?

2. How can a household serve as the basis for a new church? Why would a household be better equipped for this than any other institution?

3. Why would Jesus tell his disciples to shake the dust off their feet if the people of the town did not receive them?

4. How do you think this command applies to every disciple of Jesus rather than just those specific disciples to whom he spoke?

> *"Do not forbid him, for no one who works a miracle in my name can soon afterward speak evil of me. For he who is not against us is on our side."*
>
> —Mark 9:39

The disciples of Jesus saw a man on the road who was casting out demons in the name of Jesus. Because he was not one of their number, they told him to stop. Jesus' response is to tell his disciples not to forbid him to cast out demons. He does not want his disciples worried about who is authorized to preach the Kingdom of God or do good works in the name of Jesus. If someone does a miracle in the name of Jesus, he reasoned, he cannot speak evil of Jesus. A witness of the power found in the Kingdom of God, embodied in the person of Jesus Christ, cannot ignore the truth of the Gospel.

Jesus forbids his disciples from forbidding other people, not of their group, to do the work of the Kingdom. This is very significant for disciples of Jesus today. How many churches and sects squabble about who is really authorized to preach the Gospel rather than encouraging the Gospel to be preached? How much effort is placed on defending personal territories and kingdoms rather than propagating the Kingdom of God? Jesus will have none of it. His simple statement is: "He who is not against us is on our side." If someone uses the name and authority of Jesus to forward the work of the Kingdom of God, then let them. The goal of Jesus is the Kingdom coming on earth.

As disciples, we sometimes confuse God's Kingdom with our spheres of influence. God allows us to operate in certain areas, with certain people, in the power of the Holy Spirit. We come to think this belongs to us; it is our *right*. We have no right to anything in God's Kingdom, not if we truly believe in *grace*. Grace is the unmerited, unearned favor of God. So whatever we do for or in God's Kingdom is strictly a gift to us, only because He allows us to do it. We cannot claim exclusive rights or ownership of anything.

How this outlook of Jesus frees us from the human pettiness and squabbles! If all we thought about were His Kingdom goals, if all we fought against were obstacles to His Kingdom coming, it would save us from creating collateral damage. How many people have been injured by "friendly fire" in the battle which rages for the souls of Men? In this command, Jesus is saying we have plenty of enemies to fight as we preach the Gospel, but those who do the liberating work of God are not among them. People who heal, show forth God's glory, and point to Jesus for salvation are not against Jesus. They are on His side.

His side is our side because, as disciples, we align ourselves with Him. Jesus decides where to plant His banner and we rally to Him, not the other way around. What business is it of ours to decide who is rallying to His banner? That is His affair.

Questions:

1. Why did Jesus' disciples tell the man casting out demons to stop?

2. Why did Jesus tell them not to forbid him?

3. Why do Christians squabble sometimes about who is authorized by Jesus to act in His name?

4. When would it be correct to forbid someone to act in the name of Jesus?

5. Who decides what is to be done in the name of the Kingdom of God? How do disciples of Jesus know what these things are?

6. How does this command relate to you as a disciple of Jesus?

> *"One thing you lack: go your way, sell whatever you have and give to the poor, and you will have treasure in heaven; and come, take up the cross and follow me."*
> —Mark 10:21

Jesus gave this command to a young man who asked what he should do to inherit eternal life. The man wanted to know how he could enter God's Kingdom. Jesus initially told him he knew the commandments of God. The man responded he had kept God's commandments since he was very young. Mark's Gospel tells us "Jesus looked at him and loved him." (Mark 10:21) When Jesus sees someone who really seeks after God, someone who strives to please God in every area of their life, it is very pleasing to him; He loves them!

In fact, Jesus loved the young man so much He made an offer: sell what you have, give it away, and come follow me. Jesus made him the offer of a lifetime. He was being offered to become a close disciple of Jesus, the same as the twelve apostles and others who followed Jesus from place to place in His ministry. This was a great honor. Remember the story of the man Jesus cast the demon from and how the man *begged* Jesus to come with Him? (Mark 5:19) In that case, Jesus sent him home and did not allow him to come with Him. In this case, Jesus is offering the young man a great treasure, something the demon-possessed man wanted very badly, but could not have yet.

However, when the young man heard he would have to sell all his great wealth in order to do it, the Bible tells us his face fell and "he went away sad." What made the young man sad was the thought of giving up his wealth in order to gain what Jesus had to offer: eternal life. It was a test and the young man failed. He said he wanted eternal life, but he did not want to make the change necessary to receive such a great treasure. The response of Jesus to the young man walking away is to look around at His disciples and say, "How hard it is for the rich to enter the kingdom of God!" (Mark 10:23) Jesus made a clear distinction for them. By walking away from His offer of discipleship at one point, the man was rejecting God on all points. For you cannot follow only the commands of God which seem pleasing to you. If you want to please God by obeying His commands, if you really want an answer to your question "what must I do to inherit eternal life?", then you must be prepared in advance to do what God answers. Any denial of God's kingdom at one point is a denial of the whole kingdom. It cannot be "Jesus is Lord!" unless it is "Jesus is Lord of all." He will not be a partial master or partial savior.

Many things in life threaten us with attachment the way wealth threatened this young man. Our families, careers, accomplishments, hobbies, and interests all compete for our devotion. Let us be clear: if we wish to follow Jesus, then we will not be able to follow other things as well. We may enjoy the people, events, and circumstances of life, but we must never walk away sad from Jesus if we must give them up in order to follow where He leads. If we are to be disciples of Christ, then our attitude should instead be like the demon-possessed man, begging Jesus to go with Him. As we saw earlier, He may respond by telling us to remain in our situation. Then again, He may receive us joyfully on one of His expeditions to the frontiers of the Kingdom where we will be asked to expand its territory in the human heart.

One thing is certain, Jesus is pleased to see our desire to follow Him, just as He was pleased by the young man's devotion to the commandments of God. Jesus wants our entry into the Kingdom even more than we want it. He certainly wanted it more than the rich young man did who walked away sad. Jesus used this situation to teach His other disciples how the riches of the world and every other thing it offers can be a hindrance to us as citizens of His Kingdom.

The offer of Jesus to the young man is to "take up the cross and follow me." Jesus knew following Him as a disciple involved carrying a cross. A cross is a method of execution. So to "carry the cross" means to embrace the execution of the kind of life you thought you would have in order to discover the kind of life God has for you. Of course, Jesus does not expect us to do something which He himself was not willing to do. Instead, He invites us to join Him in carrying the cross. He wants us to accompany Him as He proceeds through death into the new life of the Kingdom of God. It is a necessary part of discipleship, this cross-carrying thing. Since Jesus carried His cross, we must also carry one if we are to walk as He walked.

For this young man, the cross was the loss of his wealth. For each of us, it will be something different, but in each case, it will be something valuable to us. We cannot embrace the treasure of discipleship until we drop the treasures we clutch so closely to our breasts.

Questions:

1. What did Jesus love about the young man who approached him looking for eternal life?

2. How did Jesus respond to this young man going away sadly?

3. Why does Jesus imply the young man did not enter the Kingdom of God?

4. How was the rich young man different from the demon-possessed man?

5. Why does Jesus say the young man must "carry the cross"?

6. Is there something holding you back from following Jesus completely? What is it? How can you deal with it?

"Have faith in God."

—Mark 11:22

Jesus gave this command to Peter after Peter was amazed to see a fig tree Jesus had cursed the previous day. It was completely withered from the roots up. This was astounding because Jesus had said nothing more than "May no one ever eat fruit from you again." (Mark 11:14) He was hungry and very disappointed to find no fruit on the tree. So you can imagine how Peter might have felt to walk by that spot and see the tree all withered up the next morning.

What Jesus answered Peter is a command to have Biblical faith. When the Bible speaks of "faith" it is not in the sense of some quality you possess. Some people think, "If only I had enough faith, then such and such would happen." What Jesus said is what is important about faith is not how much you have, but its object. Faith is quite simply, *trust*. The correct object of our trust is God. Jesus is not just commanding us to have faith, He is telling us to *trust God*.

He went on to explain to Peter if anyone says to a mountain, "Go throw yourself into the sea," and does not doubt but believes it will happen, it will be done for him. (Mark 11:23) He goes on to say, "Therefore I tell you, whatever you ask for in prayer, believe that you have received it, and it will be yours." (v. 24) What is important, Jesus said, is not how powerful is your faith, but how powerful is God. Our trust when we pray is that God will answer us. It is ridiculous to think I can say something to a mountain and it will be thrown into the sea. This is the whole point of why Jesus used a ridiculous example. He wants us to know trusting God makes all things possible because "All things are possible with God." (Mark 10:27) God is the reason why a mountain could be lifted up or a fig tree withered from the roots by simply speaking a word. How is this hard for Him since He spoke the very world into existence? (Genesis 1:3)

The lesson Jesus taught his disciples is if they will trust God, even ordinary things like fig trees can be impacted by their prayers. There is no aspect of life immune from a praying disciple. He wants us to trust God this way, the way He himself trusted his Father. Then Jesus mentioned something which seems unrelated to the point. He said, "And when you stand praying, if you hold anything against anyone, forgive him so that your Father in heaven may forgive you your sins." (v.25) Jesus tied the issue of forgiveness to our faith in God and seeing our prayers answered. If we trust God in the area of answering our requests, then we must also trust him when he tells us to forgive others. If we want to see our requests granted, we must grant forgiveness to those who have sinned against us. If we ask for the forgiveness of our sins, we must be sure to forgive others their sins as well. We will not receive what we ask of God if we refuse to have the faith to forgive as he has told us.

All of this teaching came from a simple encounter with a fig tree and Jesus' command to "Have faith in God." For Jesus, however, the issues are all related. We will receive what we ask for if we trust the One we are asking. And while we ask, if we remember we hold anything against someone, we must forgive them their offense. This clears the way for God to forgive our sins. Implicit in this is Jesus assumes one of the things we will be asking God is forgiveness of our sins. It can, at times, seem to be as impossible as telling a mountain to be thrown into the sea. But if we ask with trust in God and forgiveness toward our fellow men, we are assured even our sins are forgiven.

If our prayer is limited to the external aspects of our lives, things like fig trees, careers, money, cars, and possessions, we miss the deeper point Jesus made. God becomes a prize dispensing machine like those kept near the exits of supermarkets.

Put in your coin and get your prize. Ask God in faith to give you a wife, a husband, a car, success and you will get it. Jesus is drawing His disciples much deeper. He also indicated the kind of prayers we should be making when he tied our prayers to forgiveness. We should be asking for God to forgive our sins. Those sins mount up into a huge heap until they look like a mountain so high we cannot remember them each individually. But by asking our heavenly Father in faith and forgiving our fellow men their sins against us, we are assured to receive what seems so impossible: complete forgiveness of this mountain of debt we owe God. It is cast into the sea of forgiveness.

Questions:

1. What is Biblical faith?

2. How can we know even seemingly impossible things will be done for us if we ask God in faith? What did Jesus do that was amazing in this example?

3. Why did Jesus tie the issue of faith in our prayers with forgiveness of others?

4. How do we sometimes treat God like a prize machine?

5. How does this command indicate the kind of prayers disciples of Jesus will be making to God?

> *"Let her alone. Why do you trouble her? She has done a good work for me....Assuredly, I say to you, wherever this gospel is preached in the whole world, what this woman has done will also be told as a memorial to her."*
> —Mark 14:6,9

A woman came to Jesus while he was being entertained at the house of Simon the Leper in Bethany. She brought with her a jar of very expensive perfume and poured it on his head. Judas Iscariot (John 12:4) and some other disciples (Matthew 26:8) objected to this lavish waste of such expensive material. They asked why it was not sold for money and given to the poor since it was worth about a year's salary.

Jesus then commanded them to "Let her alone." He did not want the disciples to bother her. Then he asked a profound question, "Why do you trouble her?" This question probed to the heart of the matter. Why were Judas and some others complaining about this lavish gift? John tells us in his gospel (John 12:6) Judas did not care about the poor; instead, he was the keeper of the money bag and used to help himself to its contents. He was thinking about his lost opportunity to dip a little extra out of the offering plate!

Jesus did not rebuke the woman. Instead, he commended her for the good work and told his disciples she will become famous for this lavish act of love wherever the gospel is preached. Lavish love comes from a heart which sees something more valuable than money. The treasure of love is relationship with another. The lover will go to great lengths to show love to the person he or she loves. If we look beyond romance, we will see love has an intoxicating effect on even the most stiff people.

Most everyone understands the outrageous emotion of "being in love" attached with romance. But not everyone is aware some of the most intense love is found in friendship. This love will go above and beyond even what romantic love will accomplish in order to bless the friend. It usually does not show up as roses on the doorstep or chocolates on heart-shaped boxes. Instead, it may involve driving a great distance to visit or writing frequent letters. Time and attention are often the most valuable gifts we give and speak volumes about who it is we love.

This woman was simply loving Jesus the best way she knew how and Jesus rewarded her for it by using her as an example wherever the Gospel would be preached. His command, in this case, is for his disciples to get out of the way of such love. We are not to imped it or discourage it. We are to allow the lover to lavish the love and perhaps be amazed at its expense. God spared no expense in showing His love for us; He sent Jesus to suffer and die on a cross for us, not while we were lovable, but "while we were yet sinners." (Romans 5:8)

In a way, this woman is an example of the lavish love of God. It was appropriate she anointed Jesus at this particular time: he was about to be crucified. Jesus pointed this out by saying, "It was intended that she should save this perfume for the day of my burial. You will always have the poor among you, but you will not always have me." (John 12:7-8) If we want to show love to the poor, we will always have the opportunity. We will not always have the opportunity to show love to particular people. We may live far away and not see them very often. They may be very old and about to die.

One defining characteristic of love is it is not diminished by giving it away. Showing love to one person does not in any way lessen the love you have for another. Pouring her perfume on Jesus did not prevent the woman from feeding the poor later. For love will always accomplish its object; it will always show itself to the one loved. As disciples of Jesus, we need not be afraid of showing extravagant love for fear we diminish the love available to others. Since love is the very nature of God himself ("God is love" - 1 John 4:8), it has the self-existent creative power of God Himself. It produces something from nothing. Love is a perpetual motion, free-energy machine defying the laws of physics. It thrives on giving itself away and produces yet more to fill the void.

Questions:

1. Do you have a friend or family member you love so intensely you find yourself lavishing attention and maybe even gifts on them?

2. Why did Judas and some other disciples object to this display of love? How does this motive contrast with the motive of the woman?

3. What kinds of love can lead people to perform extravagant acts to show their love to another person?

4. How was the woman an example of God's love for us?

5. How does this example of the woman teach disciples of Jesus something important about the nature of love? Could this be the reason why Jesus said she would be memorialized for this act everywhere the Gospel was preached?

"Be quiet, and come out of him!"

—Luke 4:35

Jesus went to the synagogue in Capernaum on the Sabbath and began teaching. There was a demon-possessed man among them who cried out and announced he knew who Jesus was, "the Holy One of God!" (Luke 4:34) Jesus sternly rebuked this demon with this command to be quiet and come out.

While this command was not given to his disciples, it does show something important about how Jesus dealt with evil: sternly. Jesus did not tolerate any backtalk from the devil or any showmanship on the part of demons. He did not allow the demon-possessed man to steal the attention away from his teaching about the kingdom of God. First of all, Jesus wanted the demon to shut up. The devil does not have anything worthwhile to offer in conversation. To allow the demon to speak is to lend credence to its message. When disciples of Jesus encounter spiritual evil, we should follow Jesus' example. Do not try to argue with a demon and do not allow it to draw attention to itself.

Secondly, Jesus was concerned for the demon-possessed man. He knew it was a demonic spirit causing the man to say those things. He did not treat the man as an enemy, but the demon. Not only did Jesus hush the demon, but he also told it to come out of the man. This had the result of healing the man from demonic possession, something which had probably bound him for a long time. Because of this command, a man was made free from terrible bondage.

Disciples of Jesus should also be aware people are not our enemies. It is the spiritual evil influencing people which we oppose. We want to see people healed, restored, and full of life in Christ. Our harsh words should be reserved for the demons and we should not be afraid to tell them to be on their way. It could mean liberty for someone in terrible bondage.

As Luke relates in the rest of the story, when Jesus gave this command, the demon threw the man down on the ground, but did not injure him. It then left him immediately. The man himself was unhurt by Jesus' command and the devil was gone. Another result was the people who heard Jesus' teaching commented Jesus had displayed authority in his teaching by casting out the demon. This was not just another traveling teacher. This man spoke the very words of God. So it is with all who preach the Gospel of the kingdom of God. They are the words of God. At times, this preaching will be followed with an act of divine power working through the disciple of Jesus. It all serves to reinforce the authority of the teaching. The Gospel is true, and it is also very powerful. Even the demons know this truth.

Questions:

1. How did Jesus deal with evil?

2. How should a disciple of Jesus deal with spiritual evil when it is encountered?

3. How does dealing with evil bring freedom to people?

4. What other purpose can an act of divine power have for the Gospel?

"I say to you who hear: love your enemies, do good to those who hate you, bless those who curse you, and pray for those who spitefully use you....Give to everyone who asks of you. And from him who takes away your goods do not ask them back. And just as you want men to do to you, you also do to them likewise....love your enemies, do good, and lend, hoping for nothing in return; and your reward will be great, and you will be sons of the Most High. For He is kind to the unthankful and evil. Therefore be merciful just as your Father also is merciful."
—Luke 6:27-28, 30-31, 35-36

Here are a string of commands, all dealing with how Jesus expects his disciples to treat hateful, cursing, spiteful enemies. It's all really quite hard to swallow. We are to love our enemies. Right. How do you do this? He wants us to do good to those who hate us. Maybe have them walk all over us, too? Bless those who curse us. Let's try to find the words....

All of this is completely backwards. Loving our enemies accomplishes nothing for us. Doing good to hateful people only helps them hate. Praying for people who treat us spitefully seems a little misplaced.

Each of these impossible cases of backward behavior has one common feature: displaying the character of God. Jesus is saying God is kind to unthankful and evil people, so we should be also, if we are to be his children. If God is merciful to those who curse him, then Jesus' disciples must be also. No matter what excuse we have for why we should treat a person differently, Jesus shows us if we are going to be his disciples, then his expectation is for us to be like God.

This Standing Order also tells us something about God. He loves his enemies. He does good to hateful people. He gives and asks for nothing in return. If we ever wanted a summary statement of what God is like, this command shows his character very well. It tells us how God acts in difficult situations, with difficult people. Any concept of a vengeful, angry God will fall before this picture of his personality. If you don't like this, you don't like God as he really is.

Jesus did not tell his disciples to behave this way for practical reasons: to win more converts or put a more friendly face on the Christian religion. It really does not matter if the person continues hating you or not. Jesus still expects you to work for their good. It is not a public relations campaign. The reason Jesus' disciples bless people is because it is their nature to bless, not because it is advantageous to do good. Thus, this command is saying the same as Matthew 5:48, "Be perfect, therefore, as your heavenly Father is perfect." We are to be like God.

How impossible it all seems; how frustratingly futile! Could any human being ever hope to be this way? Would they want to?

There is one fact that may make it possible. God has declared disciples of Jesus to be righteous (Romans 4:24). This means each disciple does not begin by trying to justify himself before God. He has already been declared justified. A disciple of Jesus has a firm guarantee from God about his or her standing. This certainty of our status, dare we call it *hope* of something better, can give us the power to do good to our enemies. The evil they do us has no impact on our standing with God, cannot touch the treasure of our inheritance of righteousness. It passes by us and through us to touch things which have no bearing on what is really important to us. If our lives really are tied up with Christ, if our hope really is in him and his Kingdom, then there is no evil or curse that can harm either of those.

If someone asks me for money, I can give it to them, knowing God will always give me what I need. If another takes something from me, I can let it go without asking for it back because God guarantees a treasure of righteousness in heaven which no one can steal from me.

Questions:

1. Why does Jesus command his disciples to love their enemies, do good to those who do evil to them, etc.?

2. What does this Standing Order tell us about God?

3. Does Jesus issue this Standing Order so we will be more successful winning converts?

4. How does this Standing Order challenge my faith in God? How is your faith put to the test by it?

5. Think of someone who is your enemy. How can you do good to them?

"Your faith has saved you. Go in peace."
—Luke 7:50

A woman came to Jesus and poured an expensive jar of perfume on his feet while he was having dinner at a Pharisee's house. The woman was full of sorrow because she had lived a sinful life. The Pharisee recognized the woman and wondered why Jesus allowed her to touch him if he was a prophet, since she was a well-known sinner in town. Jesus responded to the Pharisee by telling him a story about two men who owed money and both debts were canceled. One of the men owed a large sum, while the other owed a smaller amount. Jesus asked which of the men will love the person who forgave the debt more. The Pharisee rightly answers it would be the one who was forgiven the larger amount.

Jesus pointed at the woman and declared she loved him greatly because she had been forgiven so much. She lavished her love on him with the expensive perfume and her tears because she knew she was undeserving of the amazing mercy shown to her. Jesus looked at her and said, "Your sins are forgiven." (Luke 7:48) Then he gave the Standing Order above. He told her it was her faith in him that saved her from her sins, even though they were many. His command was short and to the point: "Go in peace."

How difficult this command is to accept at times! It means we are to simply get up and go on as if nothing had happened. She gets up from Jesus' feet with the same status as the Pharisee hosting him for dinner. She walks away in *shalom*: peace, wholeness, and completeness. No longer is she a "sinner." No longer is she regarded as the wrong kind of person, for God himself has declared her forgiven and told her to go in peace.

Often, people find it difficult to receive forgiveness for their past sins. They know very well how bad their life was before. Even though they hear and understand the forgiveness of Jesus, actually *living* like you are forgiven is a different matter. It means leaving the past behind and not allowing it to haunt you. It means facing other people who know your past confident in the promise of forgiveness God has given in Christ. Even disciples of Jesus can walk around carrying immense amounts of sin baggage after Jesus has commanded them to "go in peace." Jesus does not want his disciples walking around carrying heavy burdens from the past, especially not ones he has forgiven.

The other difficulty is people around the forgiven sinner. They often refuse to accept God has completely forgiven that person. They refuse to treat the person with the same respect they desire for themselves and are afraid to think they are now considered equal with the "sinner" in God's view. Sometimes disciples of Jesus will refuse to keep company with a forgiven sinner or become angry the "sinner" has the same inheritance in the Kingdom of God.

No doubt, Jesus expects his disciples to receive his forgiveness both for themselves and for those around them. All are to "go in peace", knowing the healing power of Jesus and his acceptance makes them whole. As Paul wrote to the Ephesians (2:13-14), "But now in Christ Jesus you who were far away have been brought near through the blood of Christ. For he himself is our peace." Jesus is the reason we are forgiven, he is the reason we can be right with God. This is the same for Pharisee or "sinner." We all receive our peace through faith in him, just like the woman who poured out her perfume upon his feet.

Questions:

1. Why is it difficult at times to accept the command to "go in peace"?

2. Why do people sometimes refuse to allow a forgiven person to "go in peace"? Why would it be difficult for them?

3. What was it that saved the sinful woman? How did she show this?

4. What does it mean to "go in peace"? What does the concept of "peace" include?

"Whoever does the will of my Father in heaven is my brother and sister and mother."
—Matthew 12:50

"My mother and brothers are these who hear the word of God and do it."
—Luke 8:21

"More than that, blessed are those who hear the word of God and keep it!"
—Luke 11:28

Technically, this is not a command. If, however, you want to peer into the mind of Jesus and see who is really close to his heart, these statements offer a perfect opportunity. No one is closer to us than family. Our brothers, mother, sisters, father are all people with whom we expect to share our lives. People were telling Jesus, surrounded by a crowd, his mother and brothers were there at the edge of the crowd, waiting to see him. The expectation is he would tell people to make room for them so they could be close to him.

What he does instead is use this as an opportunity to share with the crowd who is really close to him. It is the people who hear God's word, understand his will, and do it. These people are like family to Jesus. Their claim on his affection is greater than the claim of a blood relative. This may not seem so unusual for those of us in raised in a Western culture, but for those from Middle Eastern cultures like Jesus, this was an amazing statement. Nothing in those cultures is more important than family. You take care of your family and your family will take care of you. It was expected.

Implicitly, Jesus is saying his disciples, those who hear what he teaches and put it into practice, are more blessed than even his mother. The angel Gabriel told Mary, "blessed are you among women!" As blessed as the Virgin Mary was to bear the Messiah in her womb, Jesus said people who hear the word of God and keep it are more blessed! That is the whole point of Luke 11:28. It was his response to a woman who declared, "Blessed is the womb that bore you and the breasts which nursed you!" (Luke 11:27) She was expressing what a joy it must have been to be his mother. Jesus turned this around and showed her she could have even greater joy by hearing his word and practicing it.

As disciples of Jesus, we have the opportunity to be closer than blood-brothers to him. All we must do to have this kind of relationship is hear and obey his teachings.

Questions:

1. Although this is not a command, what do you think Jesus wants from you in these statements?

2. How does he let us know the blessing awaiting our obedience to his words?

3. How do these statements help you see how Jesus feels about you as his disciple?

> *"Let these words sink down into your ears, for the Son of Man is about to be betrayed into the hands of men."*
> —Luke 9:44

Jesus tells his disciples to "Let these words sink down into your ears." This means we are to listen carefully, meditate upon what he said, let it soak into our minds. This command was given immediately after Jesus cast a demon from a boy that his disciples were unable to chase away. Everyone was amazed at the power and majesty of God displayed by Jesus. While they were marveling about this, Jesus delivered the Standing Order to let the following words sink into their ears.

Those words regarded his coming betrayal and crucifixion. Jesus warned them he was going to be betrayed "into the hands of men". They had just witnessed his divine power at work casting out a demon no one else could budge. Everyone gloried in this act. Jesus took the opportunity to remind them what kind of Messiah God had sent. He would be betrayed. He would allow himself to be given over to the power of men; men not fit to wield power in the Kingdom of God. They were men in the sense of being short of God the same way the Bible uses the number 6 to represent Man as short of the perfection of the number 7, which represents God's completeness. God created in 6 days (Man was created on the 6th day in Genesis) and completed it all by resting on the 7th day.

To get the sense of what Jesus was saying with "betrayed into the hands of men", it is helpful to remember the Beast of Revelation has a number assigned to him also. "Let him who has understanding calculate the number of the beast, for *it is the number of a man*: His number is 666." (Revelation 13:18) In other words, the Beast of Revelation represents all the power of Mankind. He represents the best Man can do, which is far short of God's complete perfection. Jesus was saying he, the Messiah who had just demonstrated the power of God by casting out this powerful demon, would be given up to the power of Man.

Jesus was pointing his disciples to a brutal fact: winning against evil came at a terrible price. It's not always going to be victory parties and celebrations like the one they were having after he cast out the demon. Just as Jesus had to go to the Cross and allow himself to be offered up into the power of Men, so his disciples should expect themselves to encounter similar crosses, similar betrayals at the hands of men. The road to victory passes through the Cross for all disciples of Jesus. He wanted us to meditate on this, let it soak into our minds, so we would not be surprised when it happens. The kind of Messiah we have is a suffering servant rather than a royal king in purple robes. The kind of salvation we have came at the price of subjecting the perfect God to the power of imperfect Man. The kind of Resurrection they witnessed and we believe demonstrated once and for all that the best Man can do to kill God is overcome by God's power to create life. These are important lessons for all disciples of Jesus to remember.

Questions:

1. What did Jesus want to sink into his disciples' ears?

2. Why would Jesus want them to think about his betrayal into the power of Man?

3. How does "the power of Man" contrast with the power of God? How does the Bible show this contrast in other books using the numbers 6 and 7?

4. What kind of Messiah has God sent us? Why would it be important to think about this?

5. What kind of salvation has God given us? Why would it be important to think about this?

6. What does obeying this Standing Order do to help us understand the kind of Resurrection in which we believe?

"Let the dead bury their own dead, but you go and preach the kingdom of God."

—Luke 9:60

Someone came to Jesus and was so excited about the possibility of becoming a disciple he declared, "Lord, I will follow you wherever you go." (Luke 9:57) Jesus turned to him and said something very discouraging. "Foxes have holes, and birds of the air have nests, but the Son of Man has nowhere to lay his head." (v.58) Jesus was essentially telling the exuberant person what it meant to be his disciple; he would be homeless. It is interesting Jesus did not encourage the person to follow him. He did not say something like, "God will provide all your needs, just come and follow." Instead, he told the truth. If you are going to follow me, then get ready to sleep in some weird places.

Immediately afterwards, he turned to another person and said, "Follow me." (v.59) This person never asked to follow Jesus, but Jesus called him. He answered, "Lord, let me first go and bury my father" (v.60) The Standing Order under examination here is Jesus' response to his statement. Jesus said, "Let the dead bury their own dead." What he meant was the people in this man's family were spiritually dead. His command is to let these spiritually dead people worry about the funeral arrangements for their own. The man Jesus was speaking to must have been a believer in Jesus. He must have wanted to be near Jesus, hear his teaching, and obey his word. Jesus knew this and gave him a further command: "you go and preach the kingdom of God."

The man was someone who understood and believed in the Kingdom. He could preach to others how to enter the Kingdom. Jesus was telling him not to worry about family obligations to people who do not care about the kingdom of God. Instead, he should be worrying about his newfound task given by the Lord, to preach the Kingdom.

Many times, disciples of Jesus will encounter reasons to keep them from doing what God has told them to do. Many of the reasons will seem good: family obligations, career goals, retirement planning. If those reasons, however, are opposed to the Kingdom purposes of God for your life, Jesus is telling you to "let the dead bury their own dead." Let people who care about such things take care of them. Your first priority as a disciple of Jesus should be to please him. If he calls you to do something and you do not do it because of some obligation placed on you by unbelieving people, your priorities are misplaced.

This Standing Order should never be used as a guilt trip to make someone perform a religious task. Do not try to manipulate people with the Standing Orders of Jesus. Instead, it is a challenge to every disciple to evaluate the priorities in his or her life. Do I know what God has called me to do? Is there something I am allowing to hold me back from accomplishing it? Is this concern uninfluenced by the values of the Kingdom? Each disciple must confront these issues, just as Jesus allowed this man to confront the issue of his spiritually dead family and make his choice.

Questions:

1. Is there something God has called you to do?

2. What concerns may be holding you back from accomplishing this?

3. How do those concerns relate to the Kingdom of God?

4. What did Jesus mean by saying, "Let the dead bury their own dead"?

5. What other command was in this Standing Order besides "Let the dead bury their own dead"?

6. What was top priority for Jesus in this Standing Order?

"I saw Satan fall like lightning from heaven. Behold, I give you the authority to trample on serpents and scorpions, and over all the power of the enemy, and nothing shall by any means hurt you. Nevertheless, do not rejoice in this, that the spirits are subject to you, but rather rejoice because your names are written in heaven."

—Luke 10:18-20

The disciples returned from a mission exuberant about having the power to cast out demons. They seemed astonished that what Jesus told them to do, they could actually accomplish! Jesus explained he was present when Satan was cast out of heaven. He was in command then and he is now. This authority he had from the beginning he transferred to his disciples: "Behold I give you authority....", he said. His disciples should not be surprised his authority is triumphant, even when acting through them. It is, after all, *his* authority, not theirs.

His command is issued within this context. "Do not rejoice in this, that the spirits are subject to you, but rather rejoice because your names are written in heaven." It is a wonderful thing to experience the power of God working through you, to see even demons subject to your will. Jesus, however, wants his disciples to be excited about something else. He tells them to rejoice because "your names are written in heaven."

To have one's name written in heaven means you are counted among God's own people; you are on the side of God. So this display of power and authority is an opportunity of reminding his disciples they are part of the winning team. It is as if they and we have been allowed to play on the Super Bowl Champion football team. We are not star athletes, we do not deserve to play on such a team, nonetheless we are allowed to experience its benefits and victory.

This is an opportunity for great rejoicing. None of Jesus' disciples went to exorcism school. They did not have the foggiest idea how to cast out demons. Yet, here they were, ordering powerful spirits to leave people alone and the spirits actually obeyed! In the same way, we modern disciples may not be the gifted or talented people, we may not feel like we know all we should or have the right skills. Even still, this does not prevent us from acting in the authority of God when we do his will. We know God wants us to share the Gospel, to pray for people, to speak the truth in a world full of lies. Often, we know we have no right to do this based upon our own miserable lives. Somehow, God has chosen us and given us authority simply because we belong to him.

What Jesus is saying is the results of our actions are not so much to be celebrated as the fact God has allowed us to be a part of his kingdom. The miracles and power of our obedience are less important than the fact we are included on God's championship team.

Questions:

1. Why were the disciples excited when they saw Jesus?

2. What exactly is the authority Jesus has given to his disciples?

3. About what does Jesus want his disciples to rejoice? Why?

4. How can this command change the way we see ourselves as disciples of Jesus?

> *"Take heed that the light which is in you is not darkness."*
> —Luke 11:35

Jesus used the analogy of a lamp to describe how a Christian life should look. He began by saying when someone lights a lamp, he does not put it in a secret place or under a basket to hide it. Instead, he places it on a lamp stand for all to see. The purpose of the lamp is to create light for people to see. The purpose of a Christian life is to create light in a dark world so people can see God and what he is really like. Because no one can see God, the way they will see His likeness is through the Christians they can see. So Jesus told his disciples a Christian must not hide his relationship with God and its effects in his life. There is a purpose for its public display.

Then Jesus went on to describe what the lamp is in our bodies. "The lamp of the body is the eye. Therefore, when your eye is good, your whole body is also full of light. But when your eye is bad, your body also is full of darkness." (Luke 11:34) Our eyes are a window into our minds. The eye is the doorway of perception for most people. It is how we focus the attention of our minds. If someone is blind, they are severely handicapped, they cannot experience the full world of perception available to most people and their minds cannot even comprehend certain concepts like color. If our eye is focused on subjects not in God's will, we quickly fall into sin. The mind will dwell upon what captures the eye.

The eye is also a window through which what is inside the mind comes out into the physical world. The mind controls what the eye dwells upon. So a spirit full of God and in right relationship with him will focus the eye upon things in God's mind. A person looking at a disciple of Jesus should see an eye directed to what is good, right, and noble.

Paul taught this explicitly to the Philippian church, "Finally, brethren, whatever things are true, whatever things are noble, whatever things are just, whatever things are pure, whatever things are lovely, whatever things are of good report, if there is any virtue and if there is anything praiseworthy – meditate on these things." (Philippians 4:8) In his parting words to the Philippians, Paul wanted to remind them of this important truth. We become that upon which we focus our eyes. This helps us understand why Jesus would tell his disciples to "take heed" the light within them is not darkness.

True, a disciple of Jesus begins with a clean slate, a soul washed clean in the Blood of Jesus. But if the disciple's eye is focused on darkness for long periods of time, the light within becomes dim or worse yet, becomes dark. It works both ways. What you focus your eye on tells a lot about what is inside your mind and what you focus your eye on also puts into your mind whatever captures your attention. If your attention is on God, on His word, His justice, excellent and noble things, then you will see your mind filled with these things in increasing measure. This is why Jesus tells us to "take heed" or pay attention to this issue.

Questions:

1. What does Jesus say is the purpose of a lamp? How does this relate to a Christian life?

2. How is the eye the lamp of the body?

3. Upon what should a disciple of Jesus focus his or her eyes?

4. How does this alter our minds?

5. What does Jesus' command to "take heed" mean then?

"Give alms of such things as you have; then indeed all things are clean to you."

—Luke 11:41

This command was technically issued not to Jesus' disciples but to the Pharisees. Still, it gives his disciples an insight into his priorities. He told them, "Now you Pharisees make the outside of the cup and dish clean, but your inward part is full of greed and wickedness. Foolish ones! Did not He who made the outside make the inside also?" (Luke 11:30-40)

Jesus pointed out the Pharisee attention to outward signs of obedience to God's Law. Along with it, he identified the inward attitudes of their hearts as sinful and directed them to consider how foolish they were to pay so much attention to the outward appearances while neglecting the inward attitudes. God, who made both inside and outside, clearly is not fooled. Then Jesus delivered the command of this Standing Order: "give alms of such things as you have."

The giving of alms is an action betraying an interior attitude. The action is to give to the poor, directly to people who really need it. It is something which has no earthly reward. Today, when Americans give money to a charitable organization, they receive a tax deduction from the government. Such was not always the case. It is a benefit, but the giving of alms Jesus commanded is not done because of the benefit of the potential tax deduction. Even today, the giving of alms in the sense Jesus meant would not be eligible for a tax deduction. He meant giving directly to a person in need; the beggar woman, the blind man, the orphan or widow who could not provide for themselves. Such giving, even today, has no reward except a heavenly one.

This kind of giving only occurs from a generous heart, a merciful man or woman who notices someone else's suffering and decides to do something about it from their own resources. The recipient of alms is in no position to reward the giver except to say "thank you". The purity of the motive betrays the purity of the heart. This is why Jesus followed the command by stating, "then all things are clean to you." The way to purity is not through observance of religious kosher laws or obligations. Instead, it comes through the heart. A pure heart giving alms to the poor shows it is already clean.

Now some people may think they can give alms from an impure motive: to gain the attention and praise of others. In this case, the purity Jesus talked about does not come from the action of giving. Remember, "Foolish ones! Did not He who made the outside make the inside also?" You cannot fool God. He is aware of the motives of the heart, the reason why the alms are given. Only the pure heart which gives expecting nothing in return is rewarded with the distinction of "all things being clean". The cleanliness comes not so much from the action as from the characteristic of the heart itself: a generous, merciful spirit. This is due to the amazing resemblance of such a heart to the very heart of God Himself, who is generous, merciful, and kind. The reward is simply recognizing the fact your character is the same as God's character. What a truly great treasure – an infinite reward! It is something which lasts for eternity and no one can steal from you.

Questions:

1. How were the Pharisees foolish?

2. What does it mean to "give alms"?

3. If there were no tax deductions for charitable giving, do you think people would give as much? If not, what would this show about their attitude in giving?

4. Why did Jesus follow up the command to give alms with the statement "then indeed all things are clean to you."

5. Where does this cleanliness come from? What does it mean?

6. Think about this statement:

   Christianity is not a religion, it is a change of heart.

   How does this Standing Order show Jesus' agreement with such a statement?

"I say to you, my friends, do not be afraid of those who kill the body, and after that have no more that they can do. But I will show you whom you should fear: Fear Him, who, after He has killed, has power to cast into hell; yes, I say to you, fear Him!"

—Luke 12:4-5

Jesus issued two commands here: one not to be afraid, and one to fear. The difference between the two is found in the objects of fear. Jesus does not want his disciples being afraid of men who hold the power of death over them. An example would be governmental authorities or in some cases, religious authorities such as the Taliban of Afghanistan or the Jewish Sanhedrin of his day. These people hold the power of the sword. They can really kill you if you go against them or refuse to obey them. They use this power to generate fear, which keeps the people in line with their wishes.

While Jesus is not saying to disrespect the government or any authority, he is saying his disciples should not be *afraid* of them. In other words, do not allow their power of the sword, the power of death to create fear in you, forcing you to bend to their will. The danger is there will inevitably be conflicts between the will of human rulers and the will of God for your life. Fear is a very powerful weapon. It was used during the Inquisition to make people toe the line created by those conducting the Inquisition. It was used in Afghanistan by the Taliban to force all women to wear the *burkha*, a total covering of the body. If a woman were seen in public without the *burkha*, she could be stoned to death. Through the use of fear, the Satanic kingdom of "principalities, powers, rulers of the darkness of this age, spiritual hosts of wickedness in the heavenly places" (Ephesians 6:12) influence your decisions. They cannot actually force you to do anything. Instead, they trick you into fearing consequences and thus get you to make a choice you otherwise would not make.

This influence can be extreme, as in the case of the Taliban, or very subtle. There is a subtle fear which a Christian student in an American public school may feel. Should they expose their faith in Christ publicly? Should they tell their friends the good news of the Gospel? Will they experience subtle discrimination because of it? The consequences of crossing the Taliban are much different, but the fear is the same. The fear is what can influence a disciple of Jesus to compromise or stay silent. It is this fear, Jesus commands us, to throw off. He said the worst anyone can do is kill your body and then they have nothing else they can hurt.

In contrast, Jesus commands if we are going to fear someone, it ought to be God. For God has the power not only to kill your body, but also to cast a person into hell. This is an eternal punishment. It goes on and on. So if the best a human being can do is kill you and that is weighed against eternal punishment in hell, it makes it much easier to resist making choices against God and his ways. Clearly, if we are going to fear anyone at all, it should be God, for he has more power than even the devil!

Unfortunately, many people today do not believe in hell. Yet, Jesus clearly taught such eternal punishment exists. He even used it in this command as a reason why the fear of Man's consequences should not cause one of his disciples to go against God. If a disciple of Jesus takes him seriously at this point, he will be much better off. For one thing, he will have a proper perspective on human authority. He will submit to it in almost every area except where it conflicts with his duty to God. Jesus does expect something from his disciples. His commands tell us how he expects us to live. If some other influence causes fear in our lives and pushes us in a different direction, the fear of God will help push us back into the will of God. While the love of God never falters toward us, our love of God at times grows dim and cold. This is when the fear of Man and his consequences can creep in to shape our decisions. By following this command of Jesus, we are empowered to remain in the loving will of God against strong and subtle opposition.

Questions:

1. Why would Jesus not want his disciples to be afraid of those who can kill them?

2. How is this command not an excuse to disrespect human authority?

3. Why does Satan use fear to influence you? How does it influence you?

4. Why did Jesus teach his disciples to fear God?

5. Do you think Jesus believed in hell? How do you think this belief can change the way you think about fear?

> *"Take heed and beware of covetousness, for one's life does not consist in the abundance of the things he possesses."*
> —Luke 12:15

Here is a warning command: "Take heed and beware". Jesus wants his disciples to beware of something he calls "covetousness". The American College Dictionary defines "covetous" as "inordinately or wrongly desirous; eagerly desirous". Another way to express this would be to say greedy, grasping, or avaricious. Almost everyone would agree this is bad, except those who agree with the character Gordon Gecko of the film *Wall Street*, who declared, "Greed is good." He understood greed as the driving force behind capitalism and therefore a good force which produced useful results in the economy.

The actual Greek word used in this scripture, however, is *pleonexia*, which means "to wish to have more". This may or may not only mean greediness. Many of us experience the wish to have more than we own. Thinking more about Jesus' command opens the possibility he is, in fact, inoculating his disciples against something more than greed. It is one thing to desire something wrongly, to know you should not have it and yet still keep your attention upon it. At least you know it is wrong. The more subtle form of covetousness is for good things.

There are many good things in life we do not have or will not have. Setting our minds on these things is as much a prescription for unhappiness as is an obsession with something we should not own. The desire itself produces a feeling of inadequacy, of insufficiency unless the thing is obtained. It is a great lie.

Jesus' following statement exposes the lie: "one's life does not consist in the abundance of the things he possesses." What we have does not define our lives. Jesus is making a statement of fact. Many people dispute this fact. Millionaires are defined by their millions, antique car collectors are defined by the quality and quantity of their collections. Even if these people define themselves by their possessions, it is a mistake from which Jesus is steering his disciples away. He knew what true life is and he said it is *not* found in the abundance of possessions.

The trick about covetousness is the collection never seems to be adequate. Once a successful acquisition is made, another possession seizes the heart and the desire for it prevents contentment until that possession is obtained. Covetousness is a never-ending revolving door of desire. If life is thought to consist of possessions, then life is like a treadmill – moving constantly but never reaching a destination.

In contrast, life in the Spirit of God is one of happiness and contentment, regardless of the external financial situation. The apostle Paul wrote, "I know how to be abased, and I know how to abound. Everywhere and in all things I have learned both to be full and to be hungry, both to abound and to suffer need." (Philippians 4:12) Life in Christ is the disciple's greatest reward. It is life independent of the size of a bank account or abundance of possessions. It is something which exists in and of itself with no reference to any external thing other than God himself. It is a relationship with God; a *living* relationship depending on nothing other than his son Jesus. Jesus wanted his disciples to know they have a life beyond what people in the world think of as defining life. He wanted us to "take heed and beware" we do not start to think the way they do and be deceived into dissatisfaction and unhappiness. God has given us the greatest gift of all – life with him forever!

Even if a disciple of Christ does have many possessions, Jesus warns the disciple not to think they define his life. This is a great danger for the wealthy. It can turn a wealthy person into something less than human. People begin to see them as only a source of money. In a sense, they turn the wealthy person into a "crack whore". All they really want from the person is the provision of their money and they are willing to do anything to get it. A "crack whore" is someone who the drug dealer knows he can exploit for sex. The whore is not a person to him, so he gives the whore crack cocaine to get sex. Similarly, some people show "love" to wealthy people in order to get what they own. They shower them with favor and affection, not because they love them as a person, but because they want to get something in return. A wealthy disciple must beware the covetousness of others as well as his own.

Questions:

1. What is "covetousness" of which Jesus tells his disciples to beware?

2. Why does Jesus say his disiciples should beware? How is his perspective different from the world's?

3. Why does covetousness lead to unhappiness?

4. What does a disciple of Jesus have that gives him or her satisfaction and happiness?

5. How can covetousness affect even a wealthy person?

> *"When you go with your adversary to the magistrate, make every effort along the way to settle with him, lest he drag you to the judge, the judge deliver you to the officer, and the officer throw you into prison."*
>
> —Luke 12:58

Here is a somewhat strange instruction from Jesus. It does not seem very spiritual at all. He is talking about the situation where someone has a claim against one of his disciples and is proceeding to take legal action. How does Jesus instruct his disciples to handle lawsuits?

Before plunging into this question, however, it is worthwhile to note Jesus says, "*When* you go with your adversary to the magistrate...." It is not a question of *if* you will go. Jesus assumes his disciples will have legal scraps like every other person in the world. Just because they are his disciples does not mean they will never have disagreements with their neighbors. Many people apply a standard higher than Jesus himself. They think Christians should be above all human concerns and never have problems with people; Christians should always be so "nice" they would never even enter into a conflict requiring legal settlement. Jesus is much more realistic. He knows that often, no matter how nice you are, there will be disagreements which require arbitration.

His advice, however, is his disciples settle the matter before arriving at the magistrate. He wants his disciples to be people who work out solutions to problems. Elsewhere, he said, "Blessed are the peacemakers, for they shall be called sons of God." (Matthew 5:9) Children of God try their best to make peace. This requires a willingness to compromise where possible. A person who digs their heels in the ground and refuses to budge in every case will not be able to come to an agreement without the magistrate's intervention. If disciples of Jesus heed this command, they will "make every effort" to settle the matter.

Making every effort does not guarantee the matter will be resolved. What it does guarantee is the disciple of Jesus will not be the one standing in the way of peace and restored relationship.

As a warning, Jesus tells his disciples the magistrate may turn the matter over to a judge and the judge may send the disciple to jail. In other words, is it not better to give some ground, even make a painful compromise, rather than possibly end up in jail because you were too stubborn to settle the dispute? Magistrates, judges, and officers all have an authority bestowed on them by God to resolve disputes. Even if they are unjust judges, their authority still carries the weight of the law. If a disciple of Jesus is to suffer imprisonment, it had better be for the sake of the Gospel and righteousness' sake, not because he refused to compromise in less important matters. Jesus said, "Blessed are those who are persecuted for righteousness' sake, for theirs is the kingdom of heaven." (Matthew 5:10) It is a blessing to be persecuted for righteousness and foolish to be imprisoned because you refused to settle a dispute it was in your power to settle.

Questions:

1. Why would Jesus give a command about something as unspiritual as a legal dispute?

2. Why does Jesus assume his disciples will encounter these kinds of situations?

3. What does Jesus tell his disciples to do before the matter comes to law?

4. In what case would a disciple be "blessed" according to Jesus to be thrown in jail?

> "Do you suppose that these Galileans were worse sinners than all other Galileans, because they suffered such things? I tell you, no; but unless you repent, you will all likewise perish. Or those eighteen on whom the tower in Siloam fell and killed them, do you think that they were worse sinners than all other men who dwelt in Jerusalem? I tell you, no; but unless you repent, you will all likewise perish."
> —Luke 13:2-5

Some people came to Jesus bearing shocking news. Pontius Pilate had killed some Jews who had come to Jerusalem to sacrifice. Perhaps they were involved in some political activity against the Roman occupation. In any case, Pilate had them killed when they came to Jerusalem. One gets the impression these people expected Jesus to be shocked and angered.

Instead, Jesus turns on them and asked if they thought these Galileans were worse sinners than others. Did they suffer this terrible fate because they were such bad people? Many times, people think bad things happen only to bad people; they get what they deserve. Of course, no one ever thinks of themselves as a bad person – only other people are "sinners."

The point Jesus makes is to force them to consider they also are sinners in need of repentance. "Unless you repent you will all likewise perish." Without acknowledging you are a sinner and turning to God for salvation, you will die just as certainly as those Galileans or the people killed when the tower in Siloam collapsed. Disasters happen, but the orientation of your soul toward God determines your life, not what happens to you. Jesus' priority is clear – if you wish to live, you need to repent.

He went on to tell a story about a man who had planted a fig tree in his garden. When he came looking for fruit on it, he found none. Immediately, he turned to his gardener and told him to cut it down because it had borne no fruit in 3 years; it was useless and taking up space in the garden. Each of us, unless we show the fruit of God's Spirit in our lives, a change in our very character, are simply taking up space in his world. He created us for a purpose: to live in his image and populate his kingdom. By refusing to bear the fruit he created us for, we are wasting the life he has given us.

God's mercy is also shown in this story because the gardener replies: "Sir, let it alone this year also, until I dig around it and fertilize it. And if it bears fruit, well. But if not, after that you can cut it down." (Luke 13:8-9) Even when there is a track record of fruitlessness, the Lord is willing to work harder, apply more grace to our lives, in the hope we will respond by bearing fruit. But the clock eventually runs out for everyone, whether Pilate kills them, a tower in Siloam falls, or death finds you in sleep.

Questions:

1. How do you think the people expected Jesus to respond to their bad news?

2. On what did his response actually focus?

3. What determines whether you live or not, according to Jesus?

4. How does the story of the fig tree relate to Jesus' admonition to repent?

5. How is God's mercy shown in this story as well?

"Strive to enter through the narrow gate, for many, I say to you will seek to enter and will not be able."
—Luke 13:24

Jesus gave this command to someone who asked him a question as he journeyed through villages on his way to Jerusalem. The person asked, "Lord, are there few who will be saved?" (Luke 13:23) Jesus did not answer his question directly. Instead, he jumped straight to the important part. How many people get saved is practically irrelevant. This is immensely relevant: will *you* be saved? It is not a matter of intellectual theological debate, but of personal survival.

Therefore, Jesus advises him to "strive to enter through the narrow gate". In other words, we should make every effort not to be dissuaded from entering the Kingdom of God through an opening that seems inadequate for the task. In addition, many "will seek to enter and will not be able." There is something about this doorway into the Kingdom of God which makes it very difficult to enter. Jesus gave a clue why this is so difficult.

"When once the Master of the house has risen up and shut the door, and you begin to stand outside and knock at the door, saying, 'Lord, Lord, open for us,' and He will answer and say to you, 'I do not know you, where you are from,' then you will begin to say, 'We ate in your presence, and you taught in our streets.' But He will say, 'I tell you I do not know you, where you are from. Depart from me all you workers of iniquity.'" (Luke 13:25-27)

The people knew who the Master was, but He did not know them. They saw Him in their streets, but did not enter into relationship with Him. They knew Him as a celebrity, but not as their Lord, even though they called Him by that title.

Instead of receiving His teaching and putting it into practice in their lives, they listened and went on about their business as if they had never heard it. They continued to be "workers of iniquity" instead of filled with the righteousness of Christ. His dismissal in the story, "I tell you I do not know you....depart from me" is an acknowledgment the relationship of the Lord Jesus with a disciple is deeply personal. He knows each of them by name.

Without actually entering into a personal relationship with Christ, one is left as simply a spectator of his celebrity or a casual observer of his teaching. A disciple is one who has heard and changed his ways from iniquity to the righteousness Jesus gave. Discipleship is a *receiving* of Jesus and His teaching. In turn, Jesus himself recognizes you as one of His own.

For those who were simply spectators, Jesus added, "There will be weeping and gnashing of teeth, when you see Abraham and Isaac and Jacob and all the prophets in the Kingdom of God, and yourselves thrust out. They will come from the east and the west, from the north and the south, and sit down in the kingdom of God." (Luke 13:28-29) All the people Jesus was speaking to were Jewish. They knew the Bible, attended synagogue, and practiced the Law. His point, however, is all of this will not get you saved. You cannot expect to enter the kingdom of heaven because you have always gone to church or you read the Bible occasionally. Abraham, Isaac, and all the prophets had one thing in common: they all trusted God personally, they had a relationship with Him, they even spoke with Him and heard His voice. When God told them to change their direction, they did, out of love for God. Jesus' further point is even Gentile peoples will come from all over the world, every point of the compass, to take up their place with the Jewish prophets in the kingdom of God. The faith of these people will guarantee their relationship to the Master, regardless of their knowledge of the Jewish Law or their synagogue attendance. This must have been shocking to the Jewish crowd to hear. What?!? You mean some Gentile will have a place with God, but I will not, even though I heard Jesus preach in my town? Scandalous, but true. The response of faith is what Jesus is saying is more important. True faith is the kind which makes changes in life to align with the teaching of Jesus.

This kind of faith is the "narrow gate".

Questions:

1. Why do you think this person asked the question about few being saved or many?

2. How does Jesus answer the question? Who is the "Master" in his answer?

3. What separates a disciple of Jesus from a "spectator"?

4. What is the point of bringing up Abraham, Isaac, and Jacob in Jesus' answer?

5. What is the "narrow gate" into the kingdom of heaven?

"When you are invited by anyone to a wedding feast, do not sit down in the best place, lest one more honorable than you be invited by him; and he who invited you and him come and say to you, 'Give place to this man,' and then you begin with shame to take the lowest place. But when you are invited, go and sit down in the lowest place, so that when he who invited you comes, he may say to you, 'Friend, go up higher.' Then you will have glory in the presence of those sitting at the table with you."
—Luke 14:8-10

"When you give a dinner or a supper, do not ask your friends, your brothers, your relatives, nor rich neighbors, lest they also invite you back, and you be repaid. But when you give a feast, invite the poor, the maimed, the lame, the blind. And you will be blessed, because they cannot repay you; for you shall be repaid at the resurrection of the just."
—Luke 14:12-14

Here are instructions for parties. Can you imagine Jesus told us how to act when invited to a party and how to throw a party? But there it is, plain as day, only a few verses apart in Luke's Gospel. These instructions are related and tell us something about the priorities of God.

First, Jesus did not condemn the practice of holding parties or gatherings. It was not a question of *if* his disciples would attend or hold parties, but *when* they do, how should they behave? What does a disciple look like when invited to someone's house? What does a party at a disciple's house look like?

Second, Jesus' disciples are human beings just like others in their culture. They interact with people in "normal" ways such as coming over for dinner or inviting others for a birthday party. Some people think Christians are above all of these things and focus only on the "spiritual" aspects of life. Jesus was very down-to-earth. He went to people's houses for dinner and attended weddings. For Jesus, and for his disciples, spiritual life occurs within the context of "normal" life, not separately.

When invited to a feast, Jesus wants his disciples to seat themselves at the lowest place, not he highest at the table. In other words, a disciple is to "go low" as far as social standing and position is concerned. Jesus pointed out someone could ask the disciple to "go up higher" and then they would have glory in the presence of everyone there. This, however, is a possible byproduct of heeding his command, not the object of it. The object of Jesus' command is to show his disciples how they are to consider the social "pecking order". The status others give you should be of no consideration for a disciple of Jesus. Instead, we are to assume the lowest place, not because it is inherently better, but because our worth is no longer determined by the social status granted by others. A disciple does not need the affirmation of other people to feel important. God has already accepted a disciple as a son of the Kingdom because he belongs to Jesus, His beloved Son. Jesus passed this loving acceptance on to his disciples when he said, "As the Father has loved me, so I have loved you. Live on in my love." (John 15:9)

Another reason Jesus may have told his disciples to go to the lowest place was because He identifies with the lowly and meek. "Come to me, all you who are weary and find life burdensome and I will refresh you. Take my yoke upon your shoulders and learn from me, for I am gentle and humble of heart. Your souls will find rest, for my yoke is easy and my burden light." (Matthew 11:28-30) Jesus cares about the "little people", the people who are pushed to the back by the crowd or those who may not be valuable in the eyes of the world. He might attend a gala celebration, but he would probably end up talking with the servants. In this command, Jesus was setting a priority for His disciples; there are people at the lowest place He wants us to meet. If our eyes were always on the head of the table, we would miss the people no one gives any attention.

When a disciple gives a feast, Jesus instructed us to invite those people who probably would not even make the invitation list for the lowest place at someone else's party. He specifically told the disciples not to ask their friends, relatives, or rich neighbors. Instead, He wants us to "invite the poor, maimed, lame, and blind." These sorts of people are not attractive; they have nothing to offer in return. This gives us a clue why Jesus would tell us to invite them. God blesses people expecting nothing in return. By inviting these types of people, disciples display the character of God. Instead of thinking about social status and how to gain it, Jesus wants his disciples to actively go the opposite direction and court those with no social standing at all. A dinner or feast then becomes a way of showing God's priorities to other people. Certainly, your friends and relatives would wonder why you have asked these poor, lame, and handicapped people to your house!

Questions:

1. Why would Jesus give a command to his disciples about attending or giving a party?

2. What is the object of Jesus telling his disciples to sit at the lowest place at a feast?

3. What reaction would you get from your friends and relatives if you invited the "poor, lame, maimed, and blind" to your house for dinner? How would you explain it to them?

4. Can you think of other reasons why Jesus may have given his disciples this command?

> *"He who has a money bag, let him take it, and likewise a knapsack; and he who has no sword, let him sell his garment and buy one."*
>
> —Luke 22:36

Earlier, we examined a command Jesus issued to Peter in the Garden of Gethsemane, telling him to put his sword in its sheathe. It led to an examination of why Jesus expects his disciples to avoid the use of violence. Using this statement alone, one would be tempted to believe Jesus expects us to be complete pacifists, to forsake violence in every circumstance. The command above qualifies this pacifism.

Jesus is telling his disciples how to prepare for their mission to bring the Gospel to the world. Earlier, he had told them not to bring any money or even a change of clothes. For some reason, at that stage of his ministry, Jesus wanted his disciples to be completely unburdened and go out proclaiming the Good News of the coming kingdom. Later, he tells them to take a money bag if they have one and a knapsack to carry items they will need on their journey. If they have no sword, they are to sell their extra clothes and buy one. What is the difference between his earlier command and this one? What has changed?

This second command came at the time Jesus is about to be crucified. The first was given during the time of his public preaching ministry. In a sense, Jesus told his disciples: "Before, I told you not to worry about providing for yourselves as best you can. But now, I am going away; I will not be with you in the same way I am now. Therefore, bring money and clothes if they will help you in your mission. If necessary, buy a sword to defend yourself." Jesus is not present with us now in the same way he was with those disciples then. Instead, now he is present among his disciples through the Holy Spirit. The Holy Spirit can provide for his disciples and can defend them against their enemies, but the way he usually works is through material causes. In other words, he does not usually make food appear on your table from nowhere. Instead, he gives you a job which provides money or he moves in someone's heart to give you money or a donation of food. The Holy Spirit is fully capable of sending legions of angels in defense of Jesus' disciples, but he usually does not operate that way. Instead, he normally works through police and law enforcement officials.

In Jesus' earlier command to Peter to "put your sword in its place," we learned one reason for this command was Jesus did not want his disciples to die violent deaths as a result of violent actions. If it is God's will for them to die a martyr's death, as he did, then they should face it as he faced his death. But not every disciple of Jesus is called to be a martyr. God does not normally want his disciples to be murdered or executed. In this violent world, evil people frequently use violence to achieve their goals. In fact, we may think violence is a trump card in life. As long as someone holds the threat of violence over your head, they can choose to extinguish you whenever they wish.

Jesus is making a provision for this by telling his disciples to purchase a sword. He will not be physically present any longer to protect them from violent people, so they will need to protect themselves. In effect, Jesus is saying there is nothing wrong with defending your life from someone who is trying to murder you. God does not want you to be murdered unless He has made it plain you are to die as a martyr.

It is interesting to note the violence Jesus advocated was very limited.

And they said, look Lord, here are two swords. And he said to them, "it is enough."
—Luke 22:38

In order to protect oneself from personal harm, it is not necessary to build up an arsenal of weaponry. Two swords are enough. Jesus was not forming a rebel army. He simply wanted his disciples to know their lives were important to him and they could defend themselves if necessary. However, he did not want them to defend him because of his special mission.

How could this command have possibly come from the same person who ordered Peter to put away his sword? Does this not seem contradictory? In the previous command to Peter, Jesus said, "all who take the sword will perish by the sword." (Matthew 26:52) As a general rule, this is true; those who use violence generally die violent deaths. It is also possible, however, to die a violent death without ever touching a weapon yourself. This is the apparent "trump card" of violence. Someone else can decide they wish to murder you through no fault of your own.

Someone who uses a sword to defend himself is in another category. He does not "take the sword" in the sense of using violence as a way of achieving his goals. He is only using the sword to stop someone from killing him. Unless he knows God has chosen for him to die at the hand of his assailant, it is against the will of God for him to be murdered. He would be negligent to not defend himself. Such passivity does not honor God, it dishonors his value of your life. Violence in such a view is extremely limited in scope. A disciple may defend himself, but he cannot think Jesus endorsed more force than is necessary to save your life. Defending yourself cannot be used as an excuse to use violence when you have not been directly attacked.

Questions:

1. How is Jesus present with his disciples today? What implications does this have for us?

2. How could violently defending yourself actually fulfill God's will? What would be His goal?

3. What is the "trump card" of violence? Did Jesus forsee this?

4. What limitations would be in effect on a disciple of Jesus in using violence?

"Daughters of Jerusalem, do not weep for Me, but weep for yourselves and for your children."
—Luke 23:28

"Remember the word that I said to you, 'A servant is not greater than his master.' If they persecuted Me, they will also persecute you."
—John 15:20

Jesus was in the midst of being led away to be crucified in accordance with the will of the crowd when he uttered these words. A large number of people followed him as he was led away and the authorities placed his cross upon the shoulders of Simon of Cyrene to carry for him awhile. Among these followers were many women who wept and mourned for him. It was an unjust punishment for such a righteous man! A prophet of God, Jesus was treated like a common criminal. The women wept because they knew he did not deserve this punishment.

While they wept, Jesus turned to them and gave this command, "Do not weep for me, but weep for yourselves and for your children." He explained a time would come when the women would say it would have been better if they had never given birth. Jesus pointed out if men committed such injustices as the one they were weeping about while he was present among them, what evil would they do when he was gone? He gave a different way of evaluating the situation. He showed an eternal perspective. Jesus did not feel sorry for himself when he suffered. Instead, he wanted the women to know it was they who needed sympathy. They were the ones in greater need, more desperate circumstances.

Jesus' prediction, of course, proved very true in historical fact. Jerusalem indeed was overthrown by the Romans shortly thereafter. Faithful Jews were persecuted to the extent many retreated to Masada, a mountaintop fortress surrounded by 10 legions of the Roman army. It is one of the most awe-inspiring sites to Jews even to this day. There, the faithful Jews performed mass suicide rather than allow their families to fall into Roman hands and become subject to pagan upbringing. Masada holds a particular place in Israeli history similar to the Alamo to Texans. Indeed, faithful Jewish people were exterminated by Rome if they resisted assimilation.

Jesus' words hold a particular meaning for his disciples even today. At times, we weep for what Jesus went through on Good Friday. What he is telling us, however, is we are the ones who deserve the tears. Injustice will be part of the world as long as sin is present. Sin will be present as long as human beings endure on the earth until Jesus returns to inaugurate the Kingdom of God in its fullness. Therefore, *we* are the ones who will endure the greater injustices. *We* will be present in times when it seems better to have never been born. Jesus' sufferings were for him alone to bear, but ours will be shared. Even our children will partake of these sufferings. In a sense, we will experience some of what God the Father did witnessing the suffering of his Son. If men did such evil in the presence of the Lord, then what greater evil will they do when they think he is not present?

His command in John 15:20 is to remember what he told his disciples, "A servant is not greater than his master." If they persecuted Jesus, they are certainly coming for us. The world thinks Jesus is gone for good. They think he may have been a good teacher, but his life ended when the Romans nailed him to the cross. Jealous religious leaders were responsible for bringing about his death, using the Romans to do their dirty work. The same kind of people exist today; people who care nothing for Jesus and his commands. Those who follow his commands are repugnant to them. If they could not stand Jesus himself, they certainly will not tolerate those who preach and teach his words.

When we meditate on what happened on the first Good Friday, it is important to keep this in mind. Jesus himself commanded it. Instead of weeping just for Jesus, we should be wailing over the sinfulness of the world which continues to this day and increases even as the human race grows. Pretending everything is fine does not fulfill the command he gave as he walked toward his execution nor to his charge to remember the same things are in store for us.

Questions:

1. How was Jesus' prediction historically true that times of severe suffering were coming to those Jewish women who wept for him?

2. How is it true for disciples of Jesus today?

3. Why will such terrible events occur when Jesus is no longer present with us in the flesh?

4. How are disciples of Jesus tempted to think everything is fine in the world? How can remembering his statement about a servant not being greater than his master help overcome these temptations?

5. Why would Jesus want us to weep for ourselves and for our children instead of for him?

> *"In the world you will have tribulation; but be of good cheer, I have overcome the world."*
>
> —John 16:33

In the previous Standing Order, Jesus instructs us to weep for ourselves and our children if we are going to weep for him. This Standing Order tells his disciples to be of good cheer, joyful and lifted up. It almost seems schizophrenic. How can he expect his disciples to weep and mourn and at the same time be cheerful?

It would help to remember his previous command was in response to the weeping and wailing of the women. He wanted to remind them *they* were the ones who needed tears, not him. If we're going to be in the weeping business, we should do it for ourselves, not for Jesus. At a funeral, people frequently weep. Some people think a Christian should be happy at the funeral of another believer because the dead person is now with Jesus. While this is true, it often misses the point of the weeping. People are crying not so much for the dead person as they are for the *loss* of the loved one. Even if the dead person is in heaven with Jesus, they will not see their friend again until their own death or the Last Day. They mourn their own loss; in a sense, they weep for themselves as Jesus instructed.

In this command, Jesus acknowledged the tribulation his disciples will have in the world. Then he went on to tell them to "be of good cheer." While we may weep for our separation from Jesus, our loss of him in the flesh and for the great sin in the world we still experience, he wants his disciples to really focus on how he has overcome the world. Everything is indeed *not* fine in the world, but Jesus has *overcome* the world. What does this mean?

We cannot deny the great sin still present in the world. In fact, it seems to have only increased in scale and scope since Jesus' day. More people have been slaughtered in the past century than in all of history combined. More ingenious methods of cruelty have been devised, more subtle ways of making evil appear good. Certainly, our world is a much more brutal and dangerous place than ever before in history, albeit more sophisticated. The Nazis found technologically advanced ways to kill more Jews, Americans perfected an atomic bomb which instantly destroyed two Japanese cities, and terrorists have perfected the art of suicide bombing.

Jesus knew and acknowledged all this. He also took his disciples to another dimension with this command from the Gospel of John. It is a different dimension in the sense all the tribulation we can experience in this world exists *in the world.* His disciples are in the world, but not of the world. They exist also in a dimension completely perpendicular to this flat sheet of paper with all the misery of humanity written upon it. This dimension is Eternity. Jesus said in John 5:24, " I tell you the truth, whoever hears my word and believes him who sent me has eternal life and will not be condemned; he has crossed over from death to life." There is a clear departure for his disciples from the plane of Death which contains the whole world. They have crossed into something much greater: eternal life. This exists apart from and independent of the world, just as God exists in and of himself, without reference to the world. The eternal life of a disciple exists in reference to God, not to the world.

Because of this, Jesus told his disciples to "be of good cheer" even in the midst of tribulation. While we weep with the world for the sin in the world, especially those for which *we* are responsible, this is not the end of the story for us. Jesus wanted us to also remember he transcended the world and all its sin. He won the victory. So while sin continues in the world and even increases its effect, there is a parallel track to history. This parallel track can only be reached by trusting Jesus as Lord, following him as a disciple. Since Jesus overcame the world and his disciples now have eternal life in him, then we also have overcome the world. Or, as Jesus said in Revelation 3:21, "To him who overcomes, I will give the right to sit with me on my throne, just as I overcame and sat down with my father on his throne."

The apostle Paul reminded the Colossian disciples of this fact when he wrote, "Since, then, you have been raised with Christ, set your hearts on things above, where Christ is seated at the right hand of God. Set your mind on things above, not on earthly things. For you died, and your life is now hidden with Christ in God. When Christ, who is your life, appears, then you also will appear with him in glory." (Colossians 3:1-4). By setting your mind on the things God sets his mind upon, a disciple can be cheerful even in the midst of persecution and suffering. For these things do not impair the purposes of God. He even used the suffering of Jesus, which women wept about, to accomplish the greatest victory in history: a bridge between our messed-up world and eternal peace with him!

Questions:

1. What does it mean to say Jesus has "overcome the world"?

2. Why would the word "perpendicular" be an accurate description of how the dimension of eternal life compares to the world?

3. How could Jesus instruct his disciples to weep for ourselves and for our children, yet "be of good cheer"?

4. How does a disciple of Jesus "overcome"?

5. How would thinking about the world cause us to weep? Why does setting our minds on things above allow us to "be of good cheer"?

"Take these things away! Do not make my Father's house a house of merchandise!"

—John 2:16

This command was given by Jesus in anger. It is one of the few recorded incidents of him being angry. His anger was directed at the merchants and officials who allowed the Temple of the Lord to become a shopping mall. They were selling cattle, sheep, and doves for sacrifice as well as exchanging money. This so angered him he actually took the time to *make* a whip of cords and proceeded to beat the shopkeepers with it as he issued this command. In other words, Jesus was not overcome by a fit of rage; it was a premeditated act of zeal. It must have been very important to him.

His command to the people selling in the Temple was "Take these things away!" They had no place in the Temple. In the Book of Ecclesiastes, it is written, "For everything there is a season, and a time for every purpose under heaven." In the same way, there are appropriate places for certain actions. The place of worship is not an appropriate place for commercial activity, even if it is to sell products for worship. Jesus was teaching an important lesson about God. The prospect of profit and the buying and selling of goods has nothing to do with God's character. God is a giver. He gives of himself freely and he expects our worship of him to be given freely. The whole commercial system is not based upon free gifts or grace. Instead, it is based on earning, dealing, and rewarding. This is not to say commerce is necessarily evil, it simply does not reflect the principles of the Kingdom of God, which are derived from the very character of God. Commerce comes from Man. Grace proceeds from God.

The more general command in its application is the second Jesus gave, "Do not make my Father's house a house of merchandise!" Here, every disciple of Jesus should sit up and take notice. Jesus said loud and clear the Church is not to be made into a place of buying and selling. The proper place for a Christian bookstore is in the mall. The proper place for worship freely given is the gathering place of the church. He tells us not to make his Father's house into a house of merchandise. Instead, it should be a storehouse of grace given out freely, a Love Foundation giving out grants, not expecting repayment. This is how the worship of the Living God takes place "in spirit and in truth." (John 4:24)

Questions:

1. Why was Jesus angry about the selling of goods in the Temple courts?

2. What separates how the church should be from the business world's operation?

"God is Spirit, and those who worship Him must worship in spirit and truth."

—John 4:24

We have seen Jesus became very angry when confronted with worship which was not true, not according to God's character. A different command gave his disciples insight to his view of real worship. While passing through Samaria, Jesus stopped at a well and spoke with a woman there. She was astounded Jesus would even talk to her because she was a Samaritan. The Jews and Samaritans had very real differences on what was the correct way to worship God. Jews believed Jerusalem was the only proper place to offer sacrifice at the Temple and Samaritans went so far as to build their own temple in their country. Jews thought of Samaritans as fake Jews. They worshipped the God of Abraham, Isaac, and Jacob, but they were adulterated with paganism and did not follow the Law carefully as did Jews. The real difference between them was about how worship should be conducted.

When Jesus told her the truth about her marital situation, though he did not know her, she realized he was a prophet and brought forth this religious disagreement. "I can see that you are a prophet. Our fathers worshipped on this mountain, but you Jews claim that the place where we must worship is in Jerusalem." (John 4:19-20) Jesus' answer said a lot about how he saw worship.

"Believe me, woman, a time is coming when you will worship the Father neither on this mountain nor in Jerusalem. You Samaritans worship what you do not know; we worship what we do know, for salvation is from the Jews. Yet a time is coming and has now come when the true worshippers will worship the

Father in spirit and truth, for they are the kind of worshippers the Father seeks. God is Spirit, and those who worship Him must worship in spirit and truth." (John 4:21-24)

Jesus carefully defended the Temple from the merchants because it was a place of worship, but it was not the actual *place* that was so important to him. Instead, it was the fact it was a place of *worship*. It would be difficult for true worship to occur there in an atmosphere of commercialism. He told the Samaritan woman her traditional form and place of worship was also off-track. The Samaritans may have used the forms of Jewish worship on their mountain temple, but they were worshipping a deity they did not know. The Jews, in contrast, knew God, not because they had a Temple in Jerusalem, but because of the salvation for which they looked forward. The Messiah was taught and preached among the Jews and every Jew looked forward to this Messiah who would usher in the Kingdom of God. Without knowing God's salvation in Messiah, without looking forward to what God had yet to accomplish, it was really impossible to know God correctly. If one cannot know the God one worships, how can one worship him?

This was a big problem for me once when I visited a Unitarian church. I sat through the service and attended a fellowship time afterwards. As we were sipping juice, I noticed a stained-glass window on the side of the building. The window portrayed three important religious symbols: a Cross, a Crescent, and a Yin-Yang. The Cross represented Christianity, the Crescent Islam, and the Yin-Yang stood for Taoism. Having read the sacred texts of each of these religions, I realized they held mutually contradictory claims about God. So I asked our host, "What exactly do you worship?" His answer was very interesting. He said, "Each worships God in his own way in whatever he thinks Him to be."

This attitude is exactly what Jesus encountered with the Samaritan woman. They were worshipping God, but had no clear notion of who they worshipped! Jesus told her it is impossible to worship God in truth if you do not know him. The way to know him is through his Word revealed in the scripture of the Jews. There, it is told of Messiah, who will come and make his Kingdom known in all the world. By knowing Messiah, we are able to worship God "in spirit and truth", regardless of our geographic location.

The Samaritan woman was intelligent. She said, "I know that Messiah is coming. When he comes, he will explain everything to us." (John 4:25) At this point in the conversation, she was exactly where Jesus wanted her to be; recognizing her need for Messiah to truly worship God. Then he made this amazing statement: "I who speak to you am he." (John 4:26) Jesus revealed to her he was, in fact, the very Messiah who would explain it all. As disciples of Jesus, we have the whole necessary body of his teaching in the Gospels. This teaches us how to worship God "in spirit and in truth."

Questions:

1. Why was Jesus angry about the commerce occurring in the Temple?

2. How is the commercial system based upon a different principle than the Kingdom of God?

3. What atmosphere should characterize the gathering place of the church?

4. What was the problem with Samaritan worship, according to Jesus?

5. Since Jesus even corrected the Jews in the Temple with a whip of cords, what was it about Jewish worship Jesus pointed to for the Samaritan woman as being correct?

6. How can Jesus' teaching about worship apply to people today?

7. How can you learn to worship God "in spirit and truth"?

"Behold, I say to you, lift up your eyes and look at the fields, for they are already white for the harvest!"
—John 4:35

The disciples of Jesus had just returned from town with dinner when they encountered Jesus at the well with the Samaritan woman. They urged him to eat, but he refused. He was still thinking about what had been accomplished through his conversation with the Samaritan woman. She obtained salvation that day because she believed in him due to their discussion. When the disciples told Jesus to eat, he said, "My food is to do the will of him who sent me, and to finish his work." (John 4:34)

In effect, he was telling them he derived sustenance from accomplishing the will of God. In this sense, he was fully satisfied by what had been accomplished at the well that day. A woman had been saved and many other Samaritans also because of her testimony. God's will of salvation for all sinners was advanced and this made Jesus stop and reflect on the encounter like someone who had just finished a large Thanksgiving feast. Then he began talking to the disciples about harvest time and gave this command.

The command is to "behold", or look at intently, the fields because they are already ripe for harvesting. Jesus wanted his disciples to look around them at the people they encountered every day and see how ready souls are to be gathered in for God. The example of the Samaritan woman shows what he was thinking about. A trip to the well turned into a gathering of a soul, salvation of a sinner, and the repentance of many in town. Jesus wants all his disciples to have this same kind of vision, the same attitude of looking for souls. He commanded his disciples to "behold" and "lift up your eyes and look".

Many times we are looking for extraordinary circumstances in which to minister the Gospel to people. Jesus told us to look for extraordinary results in ordinary circumstances. One need not create rallies and large gatherings to preach the Gospel. A trip to the market, a stroll in the park, or a wait for the bus could turn into something with eternal significance if the disciple of Jesus is aware of and sensitive to his or her surroundings. The difference is not in the venue, but rather in the beholder. A disciple who "beholds" the way Jesus commands will be sensitive to the Spirit of God telling him what to say. He will notice aspects of a situation or a person that will be prophetic. Jesus was indeed a prophet as the woman said, but every disciple of Jesus is a prophet as well because the Gospel itself is the word of prophecy for all men and women. It is the answer to every situation because every situation is, at its core, the Human situation: lost in sin, needing a savior. That savior is Jesus, the one who sat at the well with the woman, and the one who dwells in the heart of a disciple.

Jesus dwells in every disciple's heart because every disciple dwells upon Jesus, lives in Christ as a new creation. As the apostle Paul wrote, "It is no longer I who live, but Christ lives in me." (Galatians 2:20) Thus, Jesus is present at the bus stop in the disciple just as he was at the well. This may sound overconfident or downright proud. It is not. Jesus is present, but the flesh is still there as well. The disciple has a choice to obey the command to "behold" or to bury his nose in the newspaper. Certainly the disciples with Jesus in that town missed seeing the harvest field for what it was, otherwise, he would not have given this command. He wanted us to have this command so every disciple would know his priorities. Jesus is more concerned with us noticing and engaging the people around us than he is with even eating food after a long day of travel. In fact, the former was more satisfying to him than the meal his disciples urged him to eat.

Questions:

1. Why was Jesus talking about harvest fields to his disciples when they returned to him with dinner?

2. What does this command tell his disciples about his priorities?

3. What does his command actually tell us to do?

4. Why is "Jesus present at the bus stop....just as he was at the well"?

5. Have you ever felt the Holy Spirit show you something about someone in what seems to be a routine encounter?

"See, you have been made well. Sin no more, lest a worse thing come upon you."

—John 5:14

Jesus gave this command to a man he healed at the pool of Bethesda. The man could not walk because he had been ill for thirty-eight years. Bethesda was a special place; people said an angel stirred the waters at certain times and if you could enter the pool during one of those times, you would be healed. Sick persons would wait by the pool for the stirring of the water and race to get in. Unfortunately, because the man was lame, he was not able to enter the pool in time; someone else always beat him to it. Jesus noticed the man was sick a long time, so he asked him if he wanted to be made well. The man complained about his inability to get into the pool in time, but Jesus simply told him, "Rise, take up your bed and walk."

The Jewish leaders who were jealous of Jesus asked the man who it was who healed him on the Sabbath, but the man did not know. Afterwards, Jesus saw the man in the Temple and gave him this command. First, it was an encouragement for him to see his wellness, to notice what God had done for him through Jesus. On the other side of a miracle, sometimes you can forget the amazing mercy of God in granting the miracle to you. Jesus did not want the man to forget his amazing healing. Then, he went straight to the point of what he was really after: the "wellness" and "sickness" of man is determined not by our physical condition alone, but also by the condition of our spirit. The second part of the command is to "Sin no more". Jesus did not say the man's sickness was caused by his sin. He was merely telling him he should go and be aware of his sinfulness and make every effort not to fall into sin. This was more important than even his physical condition.

The fact Jesus told him, "lest a worse thing come upon you" conveys the priority of Jesus. It was bad for the man to be lame from his sickness for thirty-eight years, but it would be even worse if he used his apparent health now to live a life of sin. Instead, he was healed so he could be "well". The Jewish concept of "wellness" is included in the word *shalom*, which we often translate as "peace". It means much more, however. In addition, a life of *shalom* means "the good life" in the sense of a life aligned with God's purposes. It is noteworthy Jesus first commanded the man to note how he had been made "well" rather than to simply point out he could walk now. Jesus hinted to him to consider his whole condition rather than simply the external. A "well" life is not a life of sin. Sin is, literally, "missing the mark" God intends for us. A disciple of Jesus must always have in mind the fact his or her life is not simply to be lived for their own pleasure once they have been "saved" or "healed". Instead, the life they live now has the opportunity to be one of *shalom*; a rightly-ordered life lived before God and in cooperation with his Spirit. This command to the healed lame man is really a command to every disciple, to everyone who has experienced the grace and mercy of God.

What would the "worse thing" look like? What could happen worse than being lame? It would be good for every disciple to recall the teaching of Jesus about Hell. "If your hand causes you to sin, cut it off. It is better for you to enter into life maimed rather than having two hands, to go into hell, into the fire that shall never be quenched—where their worm does not die and the fire is not quenched." (Mark 9:43-44) If a disciple of Jesus is forgiven of sin, why should he concern himself with this command? The problem with theology is it tends to compartmentalize and systematize Jesus. The urgency of his warnings about sin are not qualified with disclaimers for disciples, they are intended for all to hear and obey. God is no respecter of persons. It does not matter who you are; pastor,

Sunday School teacher, evangelist. Sin is just as dangerous for you as for any other person. It is worse for us if we are healed and then turn to a life of sin. Our condition in this case, according to Jesus, is worse than it was before we had encountered him. The writer of the letter to the Hebrews reflected on this possibility when he wrote, "For it is impossible for those who were once enlightened and have tasted the heavenly gift, and have become partakers of the Holy Spirit, and have tested the good word of God and the powers of the age to come, if they fall away, to renew them again to repentance, since they crucify again for themselves the Son of God, and put him to open shame. For the earth which drinks in the rain that often comes upon it, and bears herbs useful for those by whom it is cultivated, receives blessing from God; but if it bears thorns and briers, it is rejected and near to being cursed, whose end is to be burned." (Hebrews 6:4-8)

Some may object this verse is not talking about a disciple who falls into sin, but only the hypothetical case of someone who "tasted the good word of God" and subsequently ignored it. Whether the verse refers to this hypothetical case or not matters little. What matters is Jesus warned the healed man, someone who had tasted the goodness of God, that sin would lead him into a worse condition than the condition which caused him to wait by Bethesda for healing. Clearly, Jesus felt something more terrible than being lame awaited him. His teaching about Hell in which he instructed all to cut off the hand which causes sin showed the "worse thing" that could come upon us is the unquenchable fire of Hell as punishment for sin. Anyone who plays with sin plays with fire, whether or not you are a believer. The disciple who plays with sin is on a very dangerous road, which could tempt him to "fall away" as the writer of Hebrews said. For ultimately, Jesus demands us to choose between sin and himself. We cannot have both. If we choose sin over him, we may actually reach the point of not caring about repentance, of embracing sin and its fruit, the thorns and briers "whose end is to be burned." Sounds a lot like Jesus' description of Hell, no?

It would be better to simply embrace his command at face value and avoid sin at all costs.

Questions:

1. Why did Jesus first command the man to "see" he had been made well?

2. How is being made "well" different from simply being able to walk?

3. Why does Jesus tell the man to "sin no more"?

4. What could be worse than being lame?

5. Why does his teaching about Hell have any relevance for a disciple of Jesus?

"Gather up the fragments that remain, so that nothing is lost."

—John 6:12

Jesus was surrounded by multitudes often as he preached and taught in the countryside. He turned to one of his disciples, Philip, and asked, "Where shall we buy bread that these may eat?" (John 6:5) He was concerned for the people. Philip sized the situation up and responded that not even two hundred denarii, quite a large sum of money, would be sufficient to feed them all even a mouthful. Andrew, another disciple, noted a young man had five loaves of bread and two fish with him, "but what are they among so many?" (v.9)

At this, Jesus told his disciples to "Make the people sit down." (v.10) He wanted the distribution of food to be orderly and everyone to feel an equal chance to have some food. Once, while feeding a large crowd of around 800 people in Haiti, I recognized the wisdom of this first command Jesus gave before he performed the miracle of feeding 5000 people. I noticed once people standing in line for food tend to become impatient and pushy until they get to the front of the line to be served. There was almost a food riot among pastors waiting for dinner! But when confronted with a similar problem as Jesus, I remembered his command and instructed the food service team to have the 800 people sit on the grass and we would bring the food to them individually. Instead of rioting for the chance to have food, the people sat patiently and waited for "table service" as if they were in a fashionable restaurant. Jesus knew exactly how to deal with large crowds!

In the miracle recorded in this scripture passage, Jesus took what food was available and turned it into a satisfying meal with more left over. My situation in Haiti was again similar. We had 800 people to feed, but our food service supplies had not arrived at the site yet. All we had were 70 chicken sandwiches to feed our crew as we set up the camp. The people had come early to our meeting. The Food Service supervisor came to me and asked what we should do. Thinking of this scripture, and Jesus' commands, I asked what food we had. She told me about the 70 sandwiches, but added they would not be nearly enough to feed all these people. Trusting in God (what else could I do?) I asked her to cut the 70 sandwiches into quarters and serve them on platters as the people sat in the grass. This was done and when everyone had eaten their fill, she came and told me we had another box of sandwiches left over—enough to feed our crew!

That day, I understood how the disciples must have felt with Jesus feeding the multitude on the grass. They were so busy serving, they had no idea what was happening. One minute they were confronted with the impossibility of feeding so many people. The next, they were obeying Jesus and passing out the meal. When it was all over, they looked around and saw fragments left over. There was no smoke, no flash of bright light, no Messiah magic show; just a crowd of people that all ate supper from one young man's packed lunch. When you are busy obeying the Lord, you will experience similar things.

What is most curious, is Jesus issued this command to "Gather up the fragments that remain, so that nothing is lost." While he performed an amazing miracle and could have made as much food as he wished, Jesus wanted to conserve and recycle the leftovers! It is a window into his thought process, this little command. God is perfectly willing to perform miracles to feed his people, but he does not overlook the ordinary and everyday things like leftovers. He was keenly interested in the details and wanted to make sure his disciples gathered the fragments and consumed them. This command speaks loudly in the face of our consumer "throw-away" culture. Business interests pressure us to throw away old items and purchase new ones, even if the old ones are perfectly serviceable. Jesus wants us to gather in what remains and use it for Kingdom purposes.

Questions:

1. What could have been the point in Jesus asking Philip where they could buy bread for the multitude?

2. How did Jesus show wisdom in handling such a large crowd of people?

3. When you are busy obeying the Lord, what kinds of experiences might you have like the disciples in this story?

4. Why would the Lord issue a command to gather the fragments when he could have simply made more?

> *"Do not labor for the food that perishes, but for the food which endures to everlasting life, which the Son of Man will give you, because God the Father has set His seal on Him."*
> —John 6:27

After his feeding of the five thousand people from three loaves and two fishes, Jesus became even more popular. Who would not want to follow him after realizing you would never have to worry about having something to eat? The people went looking for him later but did not find him. Then, they set out in boats and came to Capernaum, where they saw him. At this, they were surprised, since they knew he had not entered the boat with his disciples and there was no other boat besides theirs. They had, of course, missed the miracle of him walking on the water during the night.

When they found him in Capernaum, Jesus said something quite blunt, "you seek me not because you saw the signs, but because you ate of the loaves and were filled." (John 6:26) He called them out on their real intentions. The crowd was not interested in exploring what the miracle of the loaves and fishes meant, they wanted to get more free bread. In this context, Jesus delivered the command, "Do not labor for food that perishes, but for food which endures" (v.27). He realized they needed to be taught their need for the food which he told his disciples he had at the well with the Samaritan woman, the nourishment of doing God's will. It is fine to partake of a miracle, but even then you will still die. Better to pursue the miracle worker himself, to enter relationship with him, for this relationship endures forever.

Jesus made sure they understood it was he, the Son of Man, who would give them this "food which endures" because God the Father had put his seal on him as Messiah. All the signs and wonders pointed to this fact, not to the results of the miracles themselves. To think otherwise would be similar to reading *Moby Dick* as simply a big fish story. The depth of meaning Herman Melville conveyed through the medium of the novel would be completely missed. Jesus performed the miracles out of compassion for the real situations of people, but his miracles were not simply about their material conditions. Recall he commanded the lame man to "sin no more, lest a worse thing come upon you." (John 5:14) It is possible to experience the material miracle and completely miss the point of Jesus. He came to set everyone free; yes, free from material illness and hunger, but more importantly from spiritual poverty. Jesus himself made this point quite clearly.

It is easy for disciples of Jesus to become so overwhelmed by the miracles they experience they miss the point of how the miracles encourage deeper relationship with the Lord. Crowds can run from miracle to miracle without stopping to thank God, spend time in his presence, or simply endure a hardship with the comfort of knowing he is near. This command directs us to seek after the much better food, which leads to eternal life, and which we receive from Jesus himself simply because he is our Lord, savior, and friend. He wants us to never forget he was really after *us* all the time. The miracles and wonders were only a means to an end, like a lover giving roses on Valentine's Day. Giving roses is not the end goal. Instead, he craves closer and more intimate love with his beloved. Jesus performed the miracles out of compassion, but also as a love offering like roses.

Every disciple of Jesus should think about the miracles in their life and fall more deeply in love with Jesus. Every nonbeliever should change their mind and realize Jesus is the one who holds the answers not only for this life, but eternity.

Questions:

1. Why did Jesus answer the crowd so bluntly?

2. Who gives the "food which endures"?

3. How would you be missing the point by focusing only on the result of a miracle?

4. What was Jesus really after in his ministry?

"If anyone thirsts, let him come to Me and drink."
—John 7:37

This command was given by Jesus on the last day of the Feast of Tabernacles after he taught in the Temple. There was great controversy swirling around him. At first, he went secretly to Jerusalem for the Feast because the rulers were trying to kill him over the affair of healing a man on the Sabbath. (John 7:23) Throughout John Chapter 7, Jesus is shown disputing with people who question his identity; is he the Christ or not? Finally, he cried out in the Temple, "You both know me, and you know where I am from; and I have not come of myself, but he who sent me is true, whom you do not know. But I know him, for I am from him and he sent me." (John 7:28-29) He must have grown tired of people questioning his identity, whether he had the right scriptural qualifications or not to be Christ, as if his resume mattered more than what he actually taught. At last, he stood in the Temple and issued the command to "come to me and drink."

The Feast of Tabernacles centered around remembering how Israel had wandered in the desert after leaving Egypt. The people lived in tents during the Feast to help them remember what it must have been like for their ancestors. The whole week of sleeping in tents and teaching in the Temple culminated with Jesus making it plain to everyone what was necessary for eternal life. Water is the most necessary ingredient for life. Without water, we have dry, barren deserts. Without water, a person will die within 4 days, according to survival experts. After all the disputation, Jesus made it clear where to find the most essential ingredient for eternal life: you had to get it from him. "He who believes in me, as the scripture has said, out of his heart will flow rivers of living water." (John 7:38)

Jesus was not being mysterious. He was not referring to some mystical quality a disciple would receive. His point is he had been teaching and preaching openly throughout the Judean countryside as well as in the Temple what the Kingdom of God looked like and how to participate in it. The problem was not that Jesus was vague. The problem was even after hearing his teaching, seeing miracles, and understanding how it all pointed to God and gave him glory, some people *still* refused to believe in him. Not only did they refuse to believe, they wanted to prevent him from teaching and healing any longer publicly. They "sought to take him" (John 7:30), but no one could do it since Jesus himself did not allow it because "his hour had not yet come."

The problem is some people do not thirst for righteousness. The command he cried out was prefaced by, "*If anyone thirsts*, let him come to me and drink." Some people do not thirst. Remember, from his Sermon on the Mount, Jesus identified this as a characteristic of a Kingdom disciple, "Blessed are those who hunger and thirst for righteousness, for they shall be filled." (Matthew 5:6) The command is for those people who do thirst to obey. Jesus realized no amount of argument or convincing would change the behavior of those who do not thirst. They already think they are full and satisfied. They see no need in themselves for anything else. Why should they follow Jesus?

The command has an interesting implication. Discipleship is not just for Christians. It is not for those who have a certain religious understanding and add the person and teaching of Jesus on to it. Jesus issued the command in public on the last and greatest day of the Feast of Tabernacles in the Jewish Temple. It would be the equivalent of a Bible teacher walking into a public religious ceremony such as the Pope's annual Midnight Mass from the Vatican and issuing this call. That person would, perhaps, be known to most of the worshipers as some sort of teacher, not just a total stranger, but the venue would be similar. Thousands of people coming together for an important religious ceremony held annually hear the call to become a disciple. Another example of a similar venue would be if such a call were issued inside the walls of Mecca as Muslim pilgrims circulated there from all over the world. The call to become a disciple of Jesus was issued to everyone who thirsts for righteousness and right relationship with God. And besides simply the call, Jesus actually *offers* this satisfaction of thirst. He intends to give it to whoever comes. Not only does he *intend* to give it, the satisfaction will actually occur; "He who believes in me, as the scripture has said, out of his heart will flow rivers of living water." (v. 38) Jesus had no doubt about his ability to deliver on the promise and no question as to whether he was the one to fulfill the need. He was absolutely certain he was the answer for all who thirst.

In today's pluralistic world, this is often a point of contention. People feel disciples of Jesus are arrogant to assume he is the answer for everyone from every religion and culture globally. The problem with this view is Jesus himself issued the command. It would be fraudulent for a disciple of Jesus to offer any other way for the thirsty. There is only one person who can satisfy the spiritually thirsty—Jesus himself. His disciples are not the only ones to claim this; he himself claimed it. They are simply faithfully transmitting his words. It is as controversial today as it was then. Remember the context. Jesus was being hunted because of his teaching and people questioned his credentials to be the Jewish Messiah. When they could not silence him by force of argument, they wanted to seize him. Eventually, he allowed this to happen in the proper time. However, this command to come and drink was issued first. Jesus wanted *everyone* to know they were called and invited to drink the only refreshment available for the spiritually thirsty. He also wanted them to know it was *his* to offer.

Questions:

1. What was the occasion on which Jesus gave this command?

2. What would be a similar occasion occurring today?

3. To whom did Jesus address the command?

4. Why would Jesus use the imagery of thirsting and water to convey his idea? How does this relate to his earlier teaching in the Sermon on the Mount?

5. Why is this command a point of contention still today for disciples of Jesus?

"If anyone serves Me, let him follow Me; and where I am, there My servant will be also."

—John 12:26

Some non-Jewish people came to the disciple Philip and asked to see Jesus. Philip told Andrew, who in turn told Jesus. People besides Jews were beginning to take notice of Jesus and wished to become disciples. Jesus' answer to Andrew seemed cryptic, but it actually showed what his life and ministry were all about. In answer to the fact Greek people were seeking him, Jesus said, "The hour has come that the Son of Man should be glorified. Most assuredly, I say to you, unless a grain of wheat falls into the ground and dies, it remains alone; but if it dies, it produces much grain. He who loves his life will lose it, and he who hates his life in this world will keep it for eternal life." (John 12:23-25)

When informed about the possibility of gaining disciples among non-Jewish people, Jesus turned the conversation to the timing of his death. He knew this was ultimately where his ministry was heading, what he had been sent to accomplish. The fact Greeks wanted to become disciples was a sign to him the time had come for him to die like a seed so more grain could be produced. Jesus was sown into the ground of the Jewish culture, but the harvest of God was larger than the field of just that culture. The vision of God's Kingdom encompassed all of humanity. Unless Jesus went to the Cross, this could not occur. Instead of going to the Greeks, Jesus was saying he would die so they could come to him. His death was necessary for the people of the earth to come to the God of Israel and have a relationship with him.

Jesus also taught a lesson for his disciples in this command. Unless a disciple is willing to hate his life in this world, he will not gain the eternal life he seeks. Unless the disciple goes where Jesus went, he will not be serving Jesus' Father. "If anyone serves me, let him follow me; where I am, there my servant will be also." (v.26) Jesus was going into death to accomplish the purposes of his Father. He expects his disciples to enter their "death" to accomplish the purposes of God as well. His attitude about this is shown in the next verse.

"Now my soul is troubled and what shall I say? 'Father, save me from this hour'? But for this purpose I came to this hour. Father, glorify your name." (v.27) If I know God has this purpose in mind for me, when it actually comes down to doing it, should I ask God to deliver me from the suffering that is part of accomplishing his purpose? Instead, Jesus is saying we should ask that God be glorified in whatever suffering we encounter as we pursue his purposes in our lives. Every disciple of Jesus will follow him into the purposes of God. The "death" Jesus encountered will be encountered by every faithful disciple. Following him into the purposes of God will mean death to the purposes of the world and some of your own goals for your life. Should a disciple feel sorry for themselves because of this? Absolutely not! Jesus commands us to enter it with the same attitude he had.

The "death" we encounter will not always seem like a death. In fact, it may appear to be a success, like the Greeks coming to Jesus. From a logical perspective, Jesus' answer to Andrew makes no sense. He should have encouraged those Greeks to become disciples, he should have gathered as large a crowd of Greeks as he could and included them in his followers. This would have increased the durability of his movement after he was gone. The only problem with this line of reasoning is Jesus knew this was not the way God wanted to accomplish it. Instead, he was to die for the sins of the world and rise again. This was to be presented to the whole world so they could hear and choose to believe or not believe. It was God's way; a way demanding faith rather than simply reason.

Often, disciples of Jesus will encounter similar circumstances. Ways will present themselves which appear good, but are contrary to the way God has shown you. Stick to God's way, even when the alternatives bring either apparent success or suffering and "death". This is where Jesus is and "where I am, there my servant will be also." It is his standing order for all disciples.

Questions:

1. Why is it significant Greek people wanted to become disciples of Jesus?

2. How would this have been a sign to Jesus it was time for him to go to the Cross?

3. Was Jesus troubled about going to his death? Why did he choose not to ask to be saved from the suffering?

4. What sorts of "deaths" await you as a disciple of Jesus? With what attitude does Jesus want you to face them?

5. Many alternatives will present themselves to a disciple as they pursue God's purposes in life. Some offer apparent success and others offer suffering and pain. What should be the governing rule of a disciple as he or she makes choices in life? On what basis does Jesus want us to make our decisions?

"Walk while you have the light, lest darkness overtake you; he who walks in darkness does not know where he is going. While you have the light, believe in the light, that you may be sons of light."

—John 12:35-36

"Let not your heart be troubled; you believe in God, believe also in Me."

—John 14:1

"Believe Me that I am in the Father and the Father in Me, or else believe Me for the works themselves."

—John 14:11

"Do not think that I shall accuse you to the Father.; there is one who accuses you - Moses, in whom you trust. For if you believed Moses, you would believe Me; for he wrote about Me. But if you do not believe his writings, how will you believe My words?"

—John 5:45-46

"This is the work of God, that you believe in Him whom he sent."

—John 6:29

As the examination of Jesus' Standing Orders draws to a close, it is appropriate to look at several of them lumped together, agreeing on one common object, something very important in the teaching of Jesus. Jesus' Standing Orders were not simply commands to be executed. They were intended as a way of life, a method of interpreting the world, and a guidebook for decision-making. The most important aspect of his Standing Orders, from his own perspective, is they point to him personally. The answer for everything in life is found in the person of Jesus Christ. His commands to "believe in me" (John 14:1 and 14:11) and "believe in the light" (John 12:36) are urgent expectations. For those who are troubled, Jesus offered solace by telling them just as they believed in God, they should also believe in him. For those with theological problems needing mental answers, Jesus told them to believe he is "in the Father and the Father in me". If they found this too difficult to accept, Jesus told them to at least "believe me for the works themselves."

The point of all these urgings from Jesus is he wants his disciples to believe him, accept his teaching, and receive him as they receive God. He wanted them to "believe in the light", "while you have the light" and not wait too long, allowing darkness to overtake them. This is how people become "sons of light". According to the teaching of Jesus, we cannot "walk in light" or be "sons of light" or enter God's Kingdom unless we first believe in Jesus. He is the entry point and the final destination. If people had problems believing this, he was willing to point them at least to the miraculous works he did as a testimony he was Messiah. Only God could accomplish such things. Who ever heard of a man blind from birth being given sight? Who ever raised a dead man from the grave days after he expired? For those doubtful people, Jesus was willing to urge them from the evidence of his works, but he never bent on the necessity of believing in him as the way to God.

Faithful Jewish people may have had the argument they were only required to observe the Law as their way to God. Jesus let them know he would not accuse them to God, but the Law of Moses itself would accuse them on Judgment Day. The Law in which they trusted would also act as their accuser because they refused to believe in the one God sent and of whom Moses wrote. What Jesus was referring to was the scripture, "I will raise up for them a Prophet like you from among the brethren, and will put my words in his mouth and he shall speak to them all that I command him. And it shall be that whoever will not hear my words, which he speaks in my name, I will require it of him." (Deuteronomy 18:18-19) This, in fact, was what Jesus was getting at when he said, "This is the work of God, that you believe in him whom he sent." (John 6:29) God knew the Law would not be a way out of sin into his Kingdom. The Law could never provide salvation. At best, the Law makes a person aware of what sin is and the deep need we have for the righteousness of God. As Paul wrote, "Therefore by the deeds of the Law no flesh will be justified in his sight, for by the Law is the knowledge of sin. But now the righteousness of God apart from the Law is revealed, being witnessed by the Law and the Prophets, even the righteousness of God through faith in Jesus Christ, to all and on all who believe." (Romans 3:21-22)

Disciples of Jesus must understand Jesus himself is the beginning and end of everything in life; the ultimate purpose and goal of God's Kingdom. Simply following his commands as a new form or interpretation of the Law is not living in the Kingdom. Believing in him and following his commands out of this belief inaugurates the Kingdom of God in a person's heart. The acting out of these commands brings the Kingdom of God out from the heart into the world of flesh and blood where all can experience it. The goal and purpose of obeying these commands is that, in a sense, Jesus himself is present through the disciple. "A disciple is not above his teacher, nor a servant above his master. It is enough for a disciple to be like his teacher, and a servant like his master." (Matthew 10:24-25) The goal is not for disciples of Jesus to become spiritual gurus themselves, but to become like Jesus. This is how Jesus is present in the world during this age between his first and second coming. This begins and is realized by believing in him.

Questions:

1. How is it the Standing Orders of Jesus are not simply commands to be executed? What makes them different?

2. What is the most important aspect of the Standing Orders, from Jesus' perspective?

3. How does a person become a "son of light" or enter God's Kingdom, according to Jesus?

4. Jesus said Moses "wrote about me". What is written in the Law about him making it imperative to believe in Jesus?

5. How is simply following Jesus' commands different from believing in him and obeying his commands from this belief?

"Peace I leave with you, My peace I give to you; not as the world gives do I give to you. Let not your heart be troubled, neither let it be afraid."

—John 14:27

At the last meal Jesus shared with his disciples, the dinner called the Last Supper, he was asked many questions by them about his intentions. Peter asked, "Lord, where are you going?" (John 13:36) Jesus answered where he was going, they could not follow now. He knew he was about to die on the Cross for the sins of the world. Thomas asked him, "Lord, we do not know where you are going, and how can we know the way?" (John 14:5) Jesus answered he was the way, the truth and the life. If his disciples knew him, they knew also the way. Philip wanted to see the Father, "Lord, show us the Father and it is sufficient for us." Jesus told him whoever has seen Jesus has seen the Father. Judas (not Iscariot the traitor) asked, "Lord, how is it that you will manifest yourself to us and not to the world?" (John 14:22) Jesus answered, "If anyone loves me, he will keep my word" (John 14:23).

Then Jesus delivered this Standing Order: "Peace I leave with you, my peace I give to you; not as the world gives do I give to you. Let not your heart be troubled, neither let it be afraid." (John 14:27) It was as if he was saying, "Look, be at peace. All these questions have answers that can be found in me. I am leaving my peace with you, not the false peace of the world. Don't be troubled and afraid about the future. You know me already, don't be afraid. You have all the knowledge you need simply by knowing me. And I am leaving with you the Holy Spirit, who will teach you everything you feel like you do not understand now."

This command is for his disciples to realize Jesus was leaving with them the peace which comes from his character. It is not the kind of peace the world gives, the kind that comes through superior firepower or clever checks and balances. These are necessary when dealing with sinful human beings. Jesus is one with Father God. His character is God's character and the peace he leaves with his disciples is a lasting and eternal peace. It is founded on the kind of person he is, one who is true to his promises and never out of control. He never sins, and is never unaware of the situation. Because of this peace he leaves, Jesus tells us to not allow our hearts to be troubled. He does not want us to walk around carrying huge burdens of worry and concern about the future, our spiritual lives, or theological questions. He wants us to have his peace in us.

Jesus left us his peace, but our part is to not allow the troubles to overcome his peace in us. We are not to allow ourselves to be afraid. This means, according to Jesus, we really are in control of such things now. Before we knew him, our emotions and fear could run all over us and we could not control them. Now, because Jesus has left us his peace, we do have a way of controlling the fear. We know we have his peace, based upon his promise. By trusting him, we activate this power within ourselves. Our faith operates the control switch over our hearts. The power of this control is in Jesus, not in ourselves, but our trust in him and his word connects us to this power. It is as if an electrical circuit is completed by throwing a switch. The power is there all along, but it is not available to the light bulb until the switch is turned on. Jesus has given us both the peace and the power to appropriate his peace into our lives.

Questions:

1. How did Jesus answer his disciples' questions about the future?

2. What did Jesus want his disciples to realize?

3. What kind of peace does Jesus leave with us? How is it different from another kind of peace?

4. What is the source of Jesus' peace?

5. What part does a disciple have in this peace?

"Abide in Me and I in you."

—John 15:4

"By this My Father is glorified, that you bear much fruit; so you will be My disciples. As the Father loved Me, I also have loved you; abide in My love."

—John 15:8-9

Jesus told his disciples to "abide in me" and "abide in my love". These commands were given after the Last Supper meal when Jesus focused his disciples in on the really important things they needed to remember before he was taken from them. He did not review his entire teaching for them. Instead, he directed them to himself as the reference point. His person was to be the place his disciples would abide or dwell. His love was something they could be so sure of they could build a dwelling place in it. Nothing could shake his love he left with them. Nothing could destroy his person, even the Cross.

What Jesus told those men was all of his life and teaching are contained in his person, his character. This character, as we have seen from studying previous commands consists of love intrinsically. In other words, Jesus is *ontologically* loving, by nature of his very being full of love. Not only is he ontologically loving, he is also eternal by his very nature. By abiding in him, all disciples have a secure dwelling place. Everything else in the world can be taken away, but not your position in Jesus. "As the Father loved me, I also have loved you; abide in my love." Just as the Father shares his eternal, ontological love with Jesus, Jesus shares it with his disciples.

What does it look like to abide in Jesus and his love? One aspect of such a life would be lack of fear. If Jesus faced his own execution and torture without turning away from the purpose the Father had for him, we also can be sure to face our own trials without turning away in fear. If we abide in him, then all the deep resources of his love and strength are available to us. A disciple abiding in Jesus may also seem curiously unconcerned with aspects of life most people think are vitally important. They may not really care about which career path they take or if they meet all of their family's expectations of them. Instead, they would be more concerned with what Jesus wants accomplished, what the Father is talking to them about.

The concept of abiding is a present-tense activity. You do not abide once and then call it done. It denotes your constant position or dwelling. This means an abiding disciple is often thinking about the Lord, often speaking with him, in an active relationship with him. An abiding disciple is not a religious person in the sense of following rules. They are someone who is constantly aware of the presence of God with them. Jesus himself was constantly aware of his Father speaking to him. "I speak what I have seen with my Father...." (John 8:38) He also was aware of his Father being with him: "When you lift up the Son of Man, then you will know that I am he, and that I do nothing of myself; but as my Father taught me, I speak these things. And he who has sent me is with me. The Father has not left me alone, for I always do those things that please him." (John 8:28-29)

An abiding disciple will seek the things pleasing to God because he is with God. He is not only on God's side, he is literally *with God*. In a sense, the disciple is in two places at once. He is acting on the world stage just as all people are, in the reality of the physical universe which obeys all the laws science has revealed. On another level, the disciple exists in an eternal place outside of Nature, the place where God exists in and of Himself; the place which existed before the Universe.

That "place" is a Person. The security of this "place" is where the soul of an abiding disciple dwells.

Even though the disciple abides in this eternal "place", he or she is also active in the physical Universe. "By this my Father is glorified, that you bear much fruit." Jesus is not interested in his disciples merely existing in the eternal place with him. He is clear the Father's intention is this eternal Kingdom will touch down on earth and make a real difference in the everyday world. God is glorified when his disciples bear fruit. The fruit he is looking for are the fruits one would expect from a godly person. Apples are expected from apple trees, oranges from orange trees, and the fruit of God's Spirit is expected from an abiding disciple. "The fruit of the Spirit is love, joy, peace, longsuffering, kindness, goodness, faithfulness, gentleness, self-control" (Galatians 5:22). By abiding in Christ, every disciple will begin to bear the fruit Jesus bore. According to Jesus, this is how the Father is glorified. It is not so much our songs of praise, sermons, or good works which give God glory. Instead, he is lifted up before the world when his disciples bear the fruit of his Spirit. Then all people can see the character of God in Jesus' disciples.

Questions:

1. Instead of reviewing all of his important teachings for his disciples after the Last Supper, what did Jesus do?

2. What does it look like to "abide" in Jesus?

3. How is "abiding" a present-tense activity?

4. How is a disciple "in two places at once"?

5. How does abiding in Jesus produce noticeable effects in the world?

"You are my friends if you do whatever I command you."
—John 15:14

"Why do you call me 'Lord, Lord' and not do the things which I say?"
—Luke 6:46

"If you love Me, keep My commandments."
—John 14:15

Jesus gave commands to his disciples for specific reasons. He did not arbitrarily tell them to do or not to do things. So it is reasonable for him to expect his disciples to follow his instructions. This whole book has catalogued Jesus' instructions to his disciples and attempted to generate thought and discussion about them. The bottom line, however, is what Jesus is talking about here: will we *do* them? Will his disciples carry out his commands to the best of their ability or the ability God gives by the Holy Spirit?

Jesus told them who was really his friend—someone who does his commands. Many people like to think of themselves as friends with Jesus, many religious people especially. But when it comes to actually *doing* what Jesus asked of us, they contract a case of sudden amnesia or perhaps become expert Bible lawyers to discover new ways to justify their non-compliance. Jesus is not interested in your reasons for not obeying. He wants obedience. After all, *he* is Lord, *he* is the master, *he* is the captain of this ship we call the Church. If we are looking for guidance, we need look no farther than the commands of Jesus.

But why is it many disciples of Jesus avoid obeying these commands? As we have seen, there are quite a few commands

Jesus has issued as Standing Orders for his disciples. Why do we call him "Lord, Lord and not do the things" which he says? Perhaps it is for the same reason people 2000 years ago did not. As Jesus addressed a crowd of people following him, he told them, "A good man out of the good treasure of his heart brings forth good; and an evil man out of the evil treasure of his heart brings forth evil. For out of the abundance of the heart his mouth speaks." (Luke 6:45) This verse is directly before his question "Why do you call me Lord, Lord and not do the things which I say?" (v.46) What Jesus pointed out was we are far less "good" than we think. If we fail to follow his commands, it is because there is evil in us, which naturally comes forth rather than the good he has commanded. Our greatest need is to deal with this evil. Many Christians believe this evil has been dealt with once and for all time on the Cross by Jesus. This is true, however, it is still necessary for disciples of Jesus to appropriate that sacrificial offering for sin into their daily lives. We are not automatons responding to programming received through our religious instruction. Instead, when we believe in Jesus, he sets us *free*; free to decide to obey, or free to ignore his commands. Otherwise, we render his teaching immediately after this verse (v.46) irrelevant. "Whoever comes to me, and hears my sayings and does them, I will show you whom he is like: He is like a man building a house, who dug deep and laid the foundation on the rock. And when the flood arose, the stream beat vehemently against that house, and could not shake it, for it was founded on the rock. But he who heard and did nothing is like a man who built a house on the earth without a foundation, against which the stream beat vehemently; and immediately it fell. And the ruin of that house was great." (Luke 6:47-49)

There is a real possibility we can suffer ruin in our lives because we do not obey Jesus. Even if we seem religiously obedient to correct doctrine, we can still miss the point. Jesus wants us to *do* his teaching, to *live* his commands. In this way, we show what our hearts really love. Do we love Jesus more than the sin in our hearts? Then this will show naturally in our behavior, our attitudes, our orientation. Do we really love Jesus more than our own opinions? Then we will allow our opinions to be shaped and molded by his views on life. Do we love Jesus more than our own goals and dreams? Then we will allow our goals in life to be governed by his purposes. All of this he has made clear in his commands. Jesus did not leave his disciples wondering what was important to him. He made it very clear through teaching in specific instances as well as in stories with broader applications. While Jesus' commands are not cook-book recipes, they are a gourmet cooking course. A disciple who puts into action the things learned by studying his commands will serve up a top-quality life.

Some people question whether it is even possible to perform Jesus' commands, they seem so daunting. They are very daunting to the un-regenerated human spirit. Left to ourselves, we will always choose the easier road or the selfish path. We may think we are unselfish and giving persons, but if we asked people with daily dealings with us like our families and close associates, they would be able to identify areas where we have flaws. The point of all this teaching is Jesus has given his disciples his Holy Spirit to enable them to even overcome their human flaws. This is an incredible statement. Perfection *is possible*. The point of our lives as disciples is to experience the growing awareness of the power Jesus has set in motion in our lives through the regeneration we call being "born again". By placing our trust in him and following him as Lord, the disciple really is a different kind of person. It is a difference in quality, not simply quantity. It is not so much that our good now outweighs our bad, though it will eventually. What happens to us is our life is slowly in the process of being exchanged for his. This was *initiated* by our belief, but not completed by it. The rest of our lives is the working out of this deep truth. It is why Jesus expects us to follow his commands. By doing what he said, we are becoming what he intends.

We often experience this in real life situations. If someone wants to quit a habit, they must change their behavior for a certain length of time before it even becomes possible. For instance, if you wish to exercise regularly, you must do it for at least a month or so before it becomes a routine your body accepts as normal. By obeying Jesus, we are teaching our spirits to accept what he has taught as normal instead of what we have done all our lives. We accustom our spirits to the things of the Kingdom not by simply exposing them to its teachings, but by performing certain actions in accordance with those teachings. This is how the abstract Bible study becomes a part of real life. It is how Jesus becomes incarnated in our bodies as well as dwells in our spirits. It is how we show him we truly love him.

Questions:

1. Why is it reasonable for Jesus to expect his disciples to follow his instructions? Do you think it is impossible to do this? Do you think Jesus thought it was impossible to obey his commands?

2. Why do some people avoid obeying the commands of Jesus?

3. How does obedience relate to love?

4. Do you think it is unclear to you what Jesus expects of you?

5. How does our belief in Jesus change the quality of our lives? How does obeying his commands quantify this new life?

"A new commandment I give to you, that you love one another; as I have loved you, that you also love one another."
—John 13:34

"This is my commandment, that you love one another as I have loved you."
—John 15:12

"These things I command you, that you love one another."
—John 15:17

On the eve of his crucifixion, Jesus delivered a last Standing Order which summed up and contained every command he had taught: "Love one another." He said it was a "new commandment", "as I have loved you, that you also love one another." There is great danger in simply assuming this command as the summary of everything else and then dismissing every other Standing Order. This command is actually a general Standing Order intended to provide guidance in situations presenting no apparent similarity to the ones about which Jesus spoke. Jesus addressed adultery, religiosity, judgmentalism, a murderous disposition, and many other human situations. Not every situation is covered by his direct statements in the Bible, so he gave this summary as an aid to help his disciples discover for themselves how he thinks about every situation.

The danger comes in assuming our ideas of what constitutes "love" are what God's ideas are about it. After all, Jesus commanded them to "love one another *as I have loved you.*" He is the reference point for what the definition of love is, not our concept. So if we encounter a difficult situation, we must ask ourselves the question made famous by bracelets and other trinkets found in Christian bookstores: "What Would Jesus Do?" While wearing trinkets is not what Jesus was talking about, this question is definitely what he was describing. He wanted his disciples to use his life and love as a way of living together.

This love was often compassionate and gentle, but it could also be harsh and direct. The secret to applying this command is found in the intention of Jesus in the circumstances he encountered. When confronting religious people who refused to acknowledge he came from God, Jesus was quite harsh. As he encountered downtrodden and dismayed people, he was encouraging. His demeanor changed depending on the situation and the person he was addressing. He was always loving, but he showed his disciples *love* has many different faces. By assuming this command to love one another simply means what we want love to be is a serious error. Instead, the disciple should be asking himself, how does Jesus view this situation?

The exercise of this command is not left to the reason of a disciple alone. Jesus has also left us his Spirit. He told his disciples shortly after this command, "I still have many things to say to you, but you cannot bear them now. However, when he, the Spirit of truth has come, He will guide you into all truth; for He will not speak on His own authority, but whatever He hears, he will speak; and He will tell you things to come. He will glorify Me, for He will take of what is Mine and declare it to you." (John 16:12-14) The faith of a disciple in Jesus also includes the faith His Spirit actually will guide and teach him or her as Jesus said. Jesus said He would "take of what is Mine and declare it to you." Those things Jesus could not share with his disciples because it would have been a mental overload for them, he promised the Spirit would give. So if you do not completely understand how to apply Jesus' teaching in every situation, remember he never expected even the original 12 disciples to be able to apply his teachings correctly every time.

He gave them a summary command to "love one another as I have loved you" and then he promised the Holy Spirit would actively guide his disciples into all truth. The important part for a disciple is to *seek the truth*. This attitude of loving and seeking is what guarantees you will be able to follow his commands. When we stop loving and seeking the truth, then we begin to parse out the scriptures and take this piece and that piece we like and discard or ignore the rest. A love of Jesus demands we retain an open mind toward him and all of his teaching.

Still, this summary command is powerful in its own right. Even without the other words of Jesus, it provides a template for life in contrast to what most of the world teaches. In areas where the world does agree, everyone acknowledges the benefit of such teaching. Few people dispute it is worthwhile to take care of orphans and widows. Few would argue against making peace with your neighbor. The trouble comes in the actual application, not in the general guideline. This is where the disciple has a distinct advantage, an "inside track", so to speak. For a disciple of Jesus not only has the teaching of Jesus, but also his indwelling Holy Spirit to consult. For the disciple, Jesus is not a dead guru, but a living Lord. This is what keeps the love fresh and makes obedience to this command possible.

Questions:

1   Why would Jesus have given a summary command like this to his disciples?

2. How can focusing in on this command while excluding the others be dangerous?

3. How does the love of Jesus have many different faces?

4. What two tools does a disciple of Jesus have to follow this command?

5. What attitude can help a disciple trying to follow this very general command in specific situations Jesus may not have addressed?

> *"Until now, you have asked nothing in my name. Ask, and you will receive, that your joy may be full."*
> —John 16:24

Jesus instructed his disciples to ask the Father in his name and He would grant them what they desired. He told them they would "receive, that your joy may be full." Jesus wants his disciples to ask for what they want in his name so they can be full of joy. This joy comes from knowing you have asked in the name of Jesus and your request is granted. He did not want his disciples wondering if the Father was really on their side or not. In the previous verse (v.23), he said, "whatever you ask the Father in my name he will give you." By belonging to Jesus, a disciple is in the favor of Jesus' Father. Jesus wanted them to know this.

Until then, Jesus said they had refrained from asking God for anything in Jesus' name. Jesus had probably done most of the asking for them. But since Jesus was soon to be crucified and taken from them, he wanted them to know they had good standing with his Father as well. This is an important concept for any disciple of Jesus to understand. You are the beloved of God the Father simply because you belong to Jesus. Your performance does not enter into the equation. Even if a disciple has a miserable record of obedience or "success" in the spiritual life, Jesus wants us to know we are still beloved, simply because we are his. We have the right to "name-drop" with God. The name of Jesus is the most powerful thing we have. It is our prized possession. We should not be afraid to use it.

Peter, the disciple, filled with the Holy Spirit, spoke to the rulers of the Jewish people with these words: "let it be known to you all and to all the people of Israel, that by the name of Jesus Christ of Nazareth, whom you crucified, whom God raised from the dead, by Him this man stands here before you whole....nor is there salvation in any other name under heaven given among men by which we must be saved." (Acts 4:10,12) It is clear Peter believed the name of Jesus was the only one in all Creation given by which we can be saved. There is no salvation in Buddha, Zeus, Mohammed, Isis, or the Self. You cannot be made right with God through Freudian or Jungian psychology. Only one name has the power to wash away sins and be the cornerstone of a righteous relationship with God—Jesus of Nazareth. This is a historical name, the name of a particular man in history, the name of Peter's master.

Every disciple of Jesus is under the power of this name by virtue of being a disciple. By answering the call to follow Jesus, you have come into salvation and are following him on the pathway to heaven. This is why a disciple of Jesus should never be ashamed of the specificity of Jesus' name. He or she should never be tempted to blur the line drawn in the sand by that name. All those who cross over the line to stand with Jesus as a disciple have the right to use his name freely and enjoy its Kingdom privileges. The name of Jesus means we have access to the princely privileges reserved for the Prince of the Kingdom.

The world will always try to blur the specificity of the line and what seems to be the apparent exclusivity of Jesus' name. The world cannot acknowledge Jesus' name as the way to heaven because the world always wants to find another way, Man's way. Thus, the disciple of Jesus will encounter people who will pressure him or her to equate the name of Jesus with the teachings of some other religion or teacher. They will speak about the "Christ-spirit" dwelling in everyone, but they will not speak about Jesus Christ of Nazareth. If they do mention him, it will be only as an example of this "Christ-spirit" in the world, not as the one and only Christ. Such use of his name has no power because it is not tied to his person. The use of a name only has meaning if the full power and authority of that name is invoked.

As a citizen of America, I can travel abroad and voice my opinion to people in other countries. I can invoke the name of the United States government, but it does not carry the weight of the Federal government's authority. If the President of the United States goes abroad and speaks on a topic, invoking the name of America, it is quite different. The full power and authority of the United States government's Commander-in-Chief rests in that person. It is the same with Jesus. The full authority of God rests on him. As he said, "All authority has been given to me in heaven and on earth." (Matthew 28:18) This means a disciple of Jesus can operate in God's authority, but someone else cannot. The authority rests in the particular person of Jesus and in the power of his name. We should never be ashamed to ask for what we want and we should never be ashamed of Jesus' name.

Questions:

1. Why does Jesus want his disciples to ask for what they want in his name?

2. What did Jesus want his disciples to understand about their standing with his Father?

3. How did Peter show the power of the name of Jesus to the rulers of Israel?

4. How does the world try to blur the specificity of his name? Why?

5. Why does the name of Jesus have a special authority? How can a disciple use this authority?

> *"Peace to you! As the Father has sent Me, I also send you."*
>
> —John 20:21

Jesus appeared to his disciples after his resurrection and they were amazed to see him. His greeting was, "Peace to you!" One can almost see the smile on his face at the irony of them seeing a dead man walking again, the little humorous twist in the greeting of dreary expectations destroyed and hope reborn. His command is issued in this context and amid the same sense of humor and irony. "As the Father has sent Me, I also send you."

The command is to be sent out on a mission the same way Jesus was sent out from heaven to earth. It is a conferring of authority upon the disciples and a transfer of purpose. Jesus transferred the purpose of his mission to the disciples. They now had responsibility for accomplishing the purposes of God in the world the same way Jesus had responsibility of accomplishing what the Father sent him to do in his teaching and on the Cross. It is one thing to be given a responsibility, but quite another to have the capability to perform it. Jesus took care of both because his sending was immediately followed by an empowering command as well:

> *"Receive the Holy Spirit. If you forgive the sins of any, they are forgiven them; if you retain the sins of any, they are retained."*
>
> —John 20:22-23

Jesus told the disciples to "receive the Holy Spirit." He breathed on them to actually grant the Spirit to them, just as

God breathed on Adam in the beginning to make him a living spirit. "And the Lord God formed man of the dust of the ground, and breathed into his nostrils the breath of life; and man became a living being." (Genesis 2:7) Their part was to receive the gift of the Spirit. It is no different today. Every disciple is given the Spirit of God as a birthright of the Kingdom of God. How the Spirit is manifested in our lives depends on how receptive we are to the gift, how obedient we are to Jesus' command.

The sending of the disciples and the reception by the disciples of the Spirit are tied together. They could not accomplish the purposes of God without the power of God. What was the actual power Jesus mentioned in his command to receive? "If you forgive the sins of any, they are forgiven them". An example of this spiritual power they are to receive is the power to forgive sins. No one can forgive sins but God alone. In fact, this was one of the main problems religious people had with Jesus. "Why does this man speak blasphemies like this? Who can forgive sins but God alone?" (Mark 2:7) Nevertheless, Jesus gave his disciples this power through his gift of the Holy Spirit, so they could accomplish the purpose of God on earth: to reconcile men to Him. Reconciliation with God is not possible unless sins can be forgiven. This illustrates how the sending command and receiving command are related.

For disciples of Jesus today, the purpose of God has remained the same as for the original Twelve. We are to reconcile people to God. In order to do this, God has empowered us with a message of forgiveness of sins in the Gospel. If people believe the message, their sins can be forgiven. If they do not, their sins are retained. We are sent just as much today as they were. God has not stopped reconciling the world and he has not changed his primary method of accomplishing it through his disciples. These Standing Orders can seem to be only for a certain kind of religious leader like ordained ministers or missionaries, but the commands were given to all the disciples present in the room when Jesus appeared. Thomas, one of the Twelve, was not present in the room at the time, but Jesus sent him as well. In fact, Thomas did not even believe the others when they said they had seen the Lord, so Jesus appeared to him separately and allowed him to place his hands in his side so he would believe. Thomas went on to be every bit the missionary and apostle the others did. The point is, Jesus gave the command to his disciples and empowered them to accomplish it because he wanted them to obey. There are still people needing reconciliation with God and the original Twelve are not here to do it. Who will bring them the message of forgiveness if not the disciples living today?

This brings us to another command Jesus issued in this context. To Thomas, who did not believe the Lord had risen from the dead, he said, *"Do not be unbelieving, but believing."* John 20:27 He told him this as he asked him to stick his hand in his crucifixion wounds. So many disciples struggle believing the incredible things God has done in Jesus. Perhaps it is not difficult for them to believe Jesus rose from the dead, but it is difficult for them to believe he actually wants to use *them* to accomplish his purposes in the world as much as he wanted to use Thomas, Peter or Andrew. This command encourages us to believe the unbelievable. God has chosen *you* to carry out his will in the world. He has qualified you to do it by granting you the gift of the Holy Spirit. He has set you on watch during this period of history just as a ship's captain has placed an officer in charge for specific times of day to watch the ship. To some extent, what happens in the world depends on *you* and the choices you make every day. These Standing Orders are an attempt to help you think this way as a disciple, to consider the amazing responsibility and trust God has placed with you, to realize He has empowered you to *do something for Him.* Your life has immense purpose and meaning. Do not waste it pursuing something as small as your own personal dreams. Do not waste it pursuing the expectations of others. Waste it throwing yourself at the purposes of God. Spend yourself completely on what He has given you to do in this generation. It is not a mystery what He wants accomplished. In large part, He has told us in these Standing Orders. Our main task is to simply *believe* it and live like we believe it.

Questions:

1. How was the first command to be sent out on mission in the world a conferring of authority by Jesus?

2. For what reason did Jesus give this command to his disciples?

3. What else did Jesus command the disciples so they could actually obey the first command to be sent?

4. What example of spiritual power did Jesus grant to his disciples? Why was this necessary?

5. Do you think these commands apply to you as well as the Twelve apostles? Why or why not?

6. How does his command to Thomas to be believing challenge you as his disciple?

7. What are you encouraged to accomplish by receiving his command to believe?

"Tend my sheep."

—John 21:16

"If I desire that he remain till I come, what is that to you? You follow me."

—John 21:22

These commands were given to Peter by Jesus and are the last recorded statements by him in John's Gospel. Most likely, they do not have a general application to all disciples of Jesus, but how they applied to Peter is worth examination. Jesus had just finished asking Peter if he loved him. Each time Peter answered the question, Jesus responded by telling him, "Tend my sheep." Jesus made it plain to Peter his purpose in life was to pastor the other disciples, to tend them with His Word. This is why, later on, Peter recognized he could not spend his time serving tables and instead commissioned deacons in the church to do so.

"Now in those days, when the number of the disciples was multiplying, there arose a complaint against the Hebrews by the Hellenists, because their widows were neglected in the daily distribution. Then the Twelve summoned the multitude of the disciples and said, 'It is not desirable that we should leave the word of God and serve tables, therefore brethren, seek out from among you seven men of good reputation, full of the Holy Spirit and wisdom, whom we may appoint over this business; but we will give ourselves continually to prayer and to the ministry of the word." (Acts 6:1-4) This command to "tend my sheep" must have made such an impression upon Peter he took action regarding the food distribution situation but made sure he still had time to feed the flock by preaching. He and the other apostles did this by appointing trustworthy men to carry out the distribution.

Jesus had a specific plan in mind for Peter and he communicated it to him with a Standing Order to "tend" his Church. At the time, Peter turned around and saw the disciple John following him and Jesus, so he asked Jesus, "Lord, what about this man?" (John 21:21) Jesus gave a curious answer to Peter's question. Instead of telling Peter what he had in mind for John's future, Jesus basically told him to mind his own business by saying, "If I will that he remain until I come, what is that to you? You follow me." This is the second command above. Jesus was more concerned with Peter following his commands to *him* than he was about revealing his intentions for John.

All of us are tempted to think about how God's commands apply to other people. We analyze their situations and judge for ourselves how we think they are doing. Jesus, however, is more concerned with how we apply his commands to *ourselves*. He reminded Peter he wanted him to follow, not think about John. Jesus had just commanded Peter to "follow me" (John 21:19) and he wanted Peter to focus on this instruction. It is the same with us. Jesus is more concerned with how we apply his commands in our own life than how we apply them to others. Each of us is responsible to him as Lord; *we* are the ones who receive him as Lord when we become his disciples. Following Jesus definitely has a communal element, but ultimately we each decide what discipleship will look like in our own life. How wrong or right we are depends on the Lord's intentions for us and what he has made known to us, "For everyone to whom much is given, from him much will be required; and to whom much has been committed, of him they will ask the more." (Luke 12:48)

As you have read through this book, the Lord has spoken to you in some unique way. The same written words will generate different responses in various people. It is because God is speaking to you through this examination of Jesus' Standing Orders, not me. The Standing Orders were left for all of us, every disciple in every place and time, of every denomination or cultural background. Jesus has the same general expectations of us all. Still, he has a particular plan for you. Your job, as a disciple, is to follow the Standing Orders with the help of the Holy Spirit, trusting God will accomplish his specific purpose through you in your unique role in life. By making Jesus' commands the center-point of your every thought process, you will gradually bring "every thought into captivity to the obedience to Christ" (2 Corinthians 10:5) and discover the real meaning and purpose of your life. Even if we never become aware of our specific purpose until we can look at life in retrospect, all disciples can know they are following Jesus by following his commands. Is this not what it means to be a disciple?

Questions:

1. What was Jesus' specific purpose for Peter? How did the Standing Orders above reflect this purpose?

2. Why did Jesus not answer Peter's question about John?

3. How do these Standing Orders relate to all disciples?

4. What is your job as a disciple of Jesus?

5. How can your life still have meaning even if you never really understand your specific purpose in life?

"I run in the path of your commands, for you have set my heart free."

—Psalm 119:32

To order additional copies of this title:
Please visit our Web site at
www.pleasantwordbooks.com

If you enjoyed this quality custom-published book,
drop by our Web site for more books and information.

www.winepressgroup.com
"Your partner in custom publishing."